THE RAPE OF THE LOCK

THE RAPE
OF THE LOCK

by Alexander Pope

Edited by
GEOFFREY TILLOTSON
*Late Professor of English, Birkbeck College,
University of London*

Methuen Educational Ltd

First published 1941 by Methuen & Co. Ltd
Reprinted nine times

Third edition, reset with minor corrections,
published 1971 by Methuen Educational Ltd
11 New Fetter Lane, London EC4P 4EE
Reprinted three times
Reprinted 1984

Published in the USA by
Methuen & Co.
in association with Methuen, Inc.
733 Third Avenue, New York, NY 10017

Editorial matter © 1971 Geoffrey Tillotson

ISBN 0 423 87290 7

Printed in Great Britain at the
University Press, Cambridge

CONTENTS

INTRODUCTION

The title and opening of a poem often contain a kernel of the whole. Not so much because they summarize, as they often do, its subject matter, but because they are devised so as to anchor the wandering wits of the reader. They sound strong music, fly arresting colours, array their wares in a full light, make quick promises. There is Sidney's sonnet:

> My true love hath my heart and I have his;

there is Wordsworth's ode on *Intimations of Immortality From Recollections of Early Childhood*:

> There was a time when meadow, grove, and stream,
> The earth, and every common sight,
>   To me did seem
>   Apparelled in celestial light,
> The glory and the freshness of a dream;

there is Gray's *Elegy Written in a Country Church-Yard*:

> The Curfew tolls the knell of parting day.

And so there is Pope's *Rape of the Lock*:

> What dire Offence from am'rous Causes springs,
> What mighty Contests rise from trivial Things,
> I sing – This Verse to *Caryll*, Muse! is due;
> This, ev'n *Belinda* may vouchsafe to view:
> Slight is the Subject, but not so the Praise,
> If She inspire, and He approve my Lays.
>   Say what strange Motive, Goddess! cou'd compel
> A well-bred *Lord* t'assault a gentle *Belle*?

Pope, like the others, tells us a great deal about his poem during the impact of its first few seconds. If we read their implications, we shall be well prepared for the poem itself.

I

Those implications are found to be numerous when they are looked for.

We are promised a narrative, a narrative of towering anger and conflict, 'dire Offence' and 'mighty Contests', and, moreover, a narrative springing from what the modern world has agreed to think the most interesting of motives, 'am'rous Causes'. Then again, the poem is prompted by an occasion: actual persons, whom the poet as a person thinks well of, are intimately concerned in its inception:

> ... This Verse to *Caryll*, Muse! is due;

and in its reception:

> This, ev'n *Belinda* may vouchsafe to view.

And in addition to the social context, the poem has a literary one: for though Voltaire was amused to find as many religions in England as there were sauces in France, none of them found a niche for the Homeric muse-goddess whose aid Pope is invoking.

So much may be pointed to readily. And there is more. For surely when we read those lines we are haunted by the memory of other opening lines built up in much the same way. And we are soon turning up our *Paradise Lost* and reading:

> Of Man's first disobedience, and the fruit
> Of that forbidden tree, whose mortal taste
> Brought death into the world, and all our woe ...

Sing heav'nly Muse. . . .
And chiefly thou, O Spirit, that dost prefer
Before all temples th'upright heart and pure,
Instruct me for thou know'st . . .

So the *Rape of the Lock* is a mocking poem. That is, its
literary affiliations are of a complicated kind. We might,
for instance, say that *Lycidas*, a pastoral elegy, falls into a
simple literary context: it joins friends like-minded to itself.
But the *Rape of the Lock* is a trespasser. It joins the tribe of
the epics as Puck joins the human beings in *A Midsummer
Night's Dream*. 'I sing', Pope exclaims, arranging the heavy
singing robes of Milton about him – but his attitudes are
queered by what he announces he is going to sing; and it is
not Homer's wrath of Achilles, or Virgil's arms and the man,
or Milton's justifying of God's ways to man: it is merely
the cutting off of a girl's hair. The poem is, therefore, a
civilized one, for mockery (even in the simplest of its forms,
one child mocking another) is civilized, implying a criticism.
And here mockery is far from being in its simplest form.
Some indication of how far the poem is civilized is afforded
by a comparison between its openings and the openings of
Sidney, Wordsworth and Gray. If these poems happened to
be those which any convert to English poetry encountered
first, little of their value would be lost for the lack of a
well-stored mind. All three draw on primitive material – the
naked human heart of the lover, the common earth, the
humble dead. But it is quite another matter when we come
to Pope's high-built indoor laughter. And, moreover, that
laughter is often simultaneously hitting two objects, the great
epic form (to which Milton's *Paradise Lost* was the last great
recruit) and life itself, the characters, the well-bred lord, the
gentle belle, Sir Plume. For already the amorous causes,

however mighty the contests they produced, have been dubbed 'trivial Things', a 'Slight . . . Subject'. And yet Pope is already assuring us that his laughter is to be more a smile than anything. For what could be more polite than the compliments he has already paid?

> Slight is the Subject, but not so the Praise,
> If She inspire, and He approve my Lays.

And, moreover, if we have any doubts about the urbanity of his literary intentions, there is the verse itself to allay them. A poet who is already writing so well, so 'correctly',[1] must admire the wonders Virgil and Milton performed with versification, must be a serious admirer at what, on this occasion, he is poking his little finger at. The laughter will be silver, it is promised. And yet – not all silver. There is the title and the fierceness of the verb *assault*.

II

The reader, then, is prepared quite early in the poem for literary satire and for moral satire together with its positive counterpart, moral suasion.

The moral satire and suasion were demanded of Pope by the incident which suggested the poem. At some date in 1711, at Hampton Court,[2] the young Lord Petre cut a lock

---

[1] See Appendix C, pp. 90 ff. below.

[2] So the poem alleges, see iii. 4 ff. It may be considered that Pope, when versifying a commissioned incident, would be bound to preserve so important an element as place. On the other hand, if the lock had been cut at a private house, Pope may have felt that the epic mockery demanded a voyage up a famous river, and a famous, indeed a royal house, like the palace of Penelope in the *Odyssey* or of Satan in *Paradise Lost*. Of the two alternatives the former seems the likelier.

from the head of his distant relative Arabella Fermor, a young lady renowned for her beauty. The story and its repercussions among the Roman Catholic families grouped around it, Pope was later to recount for the benefit of his friend Joseph Spence:

> The stealing of Miss Belle Fermor's hair, was taken too seriously, and caused an estrangement between the two families, though they had lived so long in great friendship before. A common acquaintance and well-wisher to both [i.e., John Caryll, Pope's friend and patron], desired me to write a poem to make a jest of it, and laugh them together again. It was with this view that I wrote the Rape of the Lock.

Pope, who was 22 and 23 in 1711, wrote the commissioned poem 'fast', in 'less than a fortnight's time', and (again according to Spence's account) it was 'well received, and had its effect in the two families'. The Fermors were again charmed with the Petres, and the beneficent Caryll charmed with both. When, however, in May 1712, print was sub-stituted for the comparative privacy of Pope's official manu-script (and for those few copies which the pleased Arabella, and the pleased author, seem to have given out to friends), the Fermor faction bristled up once more – and this although no name appeared in the poem, except the cryptic 'C——l', and no name of any author on the title-page. We find Pope informing Caryll's son that Sir George Browne, Arabella's mother's cousin, was only too fully confirming the character given him by the poem: 'Sir Plume blusters, I hear.' And, though no one else went so far as to be angry, Pope is surprised to find that 'the celebrated lady herself is offended', and offended at him. Her annoyance is difficult to account for on internal evidence, especially since, in dedicating the second and enlarged edition to her, Pope, looking back, says that the first appeared with her consent. It scarcely seems likely that this statement can be fabrication when Pope's addressee knew the facts and could have contradicted him roundly. But the consent Pope claims to have had from her may have been bestowed in the already gloomy knowledge that publication would bring discomfort. For the context implies that her choice did not lie between publication and non-publication, but only between two forms of publication, authorized and unauthorized. Of the two, she would naturally prefer the former: over an unauthorized edition she could have had no control whatever. But, no doubt, she would most have preferred to let the poem gather dust in the drawer since, less than two months before publication, Lord Petre had married another lady several years younger than she and very much richer. If Arabella had had dreams of seeing herself as Lady Petre,[1] she would quite reasonably be offended at a poem which talked of amorous causes and in subtle ways showed her ready to respond to the Baron's advances. But since no names were mentioned, her annoyance cannot have been at the mercy of every Tom, Dick, and Harry (or Meg, Sue, and Polly), though of course 'fools . . . talked and fools . . . heard them'.

III

Arabella's taking offence in this way indicates that she had failed to respond to the moral of the poem. That moral was seriously meant. Critics of the time considered the old poets had planted a firm moral in their epics and this element Boileau, Garth, and Pope imitated without mockery.

[1] Cf. i. 83 ff. in the enlarged edition.

Pope, indeed, set such store by his moral that in the edition of 1717 he allotted Clarissa a long speech setting it out so clearly that no one could have any excuse for missing it. Dr. Johnson took Pope's moral seriously and preferred its potential efficacy to that of Boileau's:

> The purpose of [Pope] is, as he tells us, to laugh at 'the little unguarded follies of the female sex' [that of Boileau being to expose 'the pride and discord of the clergy']. Perhaps neither Pope nor Boileau has made the world much better than he found it; but if they had both succeeded, it were easy to tell who would have deserved most from publick gratitude. The freaks, and humours, and spleen, and vanity of women, as they embroil families in discord and fill houses with disquiet, do more to obstruct the happiness of life in a year than the ambition of the clergy in many centuries. It has been well observed that the misery of man proceeds not from any single crush of overwhelming evil, but from small vexations continually repeated.

The moral, however, was amply clear in the 1712 version, though it often operated upside down as satire. In the 1712 version the moral was mainly to be inferred from such lines as

> Not louder Shrieks by Dames to Heav'n are cast,
> When Husbands die, or *Lap-dogs* breathe their last.

In the final poem there was the straight talking – or was it nearer to a whisper? – of Clarissa:

> And trust me, Dear! good Humour can prevail,
> When Airs, and Flights, and Screams, and Scolding fail . . .

Arabella in 1712, perhaps, did not trouble to make the hoped-for inference. And when the occasion for taking offence at the publication of the poem passed over, she is found erring again, this time on the other side – her niece, the abbess of a convent in Paris, asserted that 'Mr. Pope's praise made her ... very troublesome and conceited'. The moral of the poem did not ask much: but evidently it asked too much. And yet Pope himself had use for other things than his moral. He was a weak human being as well as a moralist and when he saw the gay and smiling Belinda launching on the bosom of the silver Thames, he saw that much must be forgiven her:

> If to her share some Female Errors fall,
> Look on her Face, and you'll forgive 'em all.

So he could say in the 1712 version and by 1714 he had gone one further:

> If to her share some Female Errors fall,
> Look on her Face, and you'll forget 'em all.

Pope dubbed the cutting of the lock a 'trivial Thing', but contradicted this in the dedicatory epistle: 'the Loss of your Hair, which I always mention with Reverence'. Beauty such as Arabella's could, he admitted, end by bemusing his philosophy.

IV

Pope wrote his poem for an occasion, for a small fashionable group. But he had another group in mind, his educated contemporaries. It was really for their sake that he dared to clap Sir Plume into the middle of the poem, rousing with his left hand the ill-feeling which he was engaged on calming with his right. And it was for their sake that the poem was a masterpiece, was indeed the chief masterpiece, of the mock-heroic. The subtleties of the poem as a mocking poem, we may be sure, were lost on the Fermors and the Petres,[1] but not on Swift, Addison, Gay, and Garth and some of the members of the larger circle who, when the poem appeared in its enlarged form, bought it to the tune of 3,000 copies in four days. It was for these that – however Belinda might wince at publication – the poem was published.

It seems that mockery of the epic manner is as old as the epic manner itself, and when Pope undertook it he was completing a process which in extant writings began with the Homeric *Battle of the Frogs and Mice*. Burlesque and mock-heroic had become especially popular in the seventeenth century – *Don Quixote* itself had appeared in 1605–15 – and, so far as Pope's particular poem is concerned, there had been Boileau's *Lutrin* (which inflated to mock-epic dignity a dispute over the placing of a pulpit) and Garth's *Dispensary* (which did the same for a dispute over the free distribution of drugs to the poor). Pope, accordingly, was doing nothing new, except that, as always, he was improving on what had just been done. Boileau and Garth had laid down the principles for effective mock-heroic, leaving to Pope the chance to produce something better by pushing the same principles to their logical conclusions of completeness, proportion, delicacy, homogeneity.

The *Rape of the Lock* is the masterpiece of the mock-heroic because in its 1714 form it mocks at the maximum amount of the epic. The mockery takes different forms, employs different devices. Apart from the general mockery of the epic form and substance – the epic manner with its

---

[1] From Pope's dedicatory epistle we could assume that Pope assumed that Belinda missed most of the literary point.

invocations, its similes, its 'He said's' and the epic matter with its machinery,[1] its battles, its journeys on water and down to the underworld, its harangues – apart from all this, there is particular mockery of a scene or a detail or a certain speech or a comment in the person of the poet. And the scale of the mimicry is always varying. We find Belinda flashing lightning from her eyes (as, in Cowley's epic *Davideis*, Saul flashes it) and screaming (like the Homeric heroes); but against the bulk of Hector, she is a mere slip of a girl, a mere fashionable lady like any figuring in the unheroic pages of the *Spectator*. We find an altar at which ardent prayers are fatefully half-granted and a goddess who is worshipped; but the altar is built of French romances and the goddess is the image of the vain Belinda in the mirror of her dressing-table. We find a battle drawn forth to combat, like the Greeks, on a velvet plain; but it is only a game of cards on a fashionable card-table. We find a supernatural being threatening his inferiors with torture; but it is a sylph, not Jove, and the tortures are neither thunderbolts nor pains of Hades, but cruelties devised ingeniously from the requisites of the toilet table. The scale of the imitation is always shifting. But on the whole it is one of diminution. The epic is a long poem; the *Rape of the Lock* is short. The story of the epic covers years; that of the *Rape of the Lock* hours. The gods of the epic are stupendous creatures; Pope's sylphs tiny.

Pope says in the dedicatory epistle that he published before he had 'executed half [his] Design'. Certainly the poem needed to be written quickly; otherwise, the request of his patron would be left in the air, the breach between the two families would close of itself or would widen into settled

[1] Pope defines the term for Belinda's benefit at p. 26 below.

antipathy (both events making Pope's poem an impertinence). Pope may, therefore, be representing the fact truly when he implies that from the start he had designed the poem in a form which the urgency of the occasion made impracticable. But he made the earlier poem a complete thing in itself (so complete that Addison pronounced it *merum sal* and advised against enlargement), and this successful second-best may have induced Pope to postpone or abandon his major scheme until, in the end, the poem reached and passed the brink of print without their benefit. The early version was a complete thing and Pope is mistaken when he says that 'the *Machinery* was entirely wanting to compleat it', Addison, indeed, having used the poem as an instance of how to use machinery properly.[1]

Pope, like any epic poet, had already made the action of his poem take place on the knees of the gods: it was Heaven and 'the Pow'rs' which, granting half the Baron's prayer, wrested from his fingers the lock they had allowed him to cut. But from the start it must have been obvious to Pope that the epics usually allotted their celestials more room and colour than his own poem did, and his literary mockery accordingly gained in quality as the supernatural machinery gained in quantity.

In making the additions, which range from a single couplet to passages of almost a hundred lines, Pope cleverly saw to it that the sylphs were not simply added like shining trinkets and threepenny-bits to a Christmas pudding, but made to develop and flavour the whole.

The additions improve the literary mockery; and they also improve the human mockery. Ariel, for all his knowing sophistication, has something the air of a visitor from

[1] *Spectator*, 523.

Mars, showing up earthly lack of values as if by lack of experience:

> Whether the Nymph shall break *Diana*'s Law,
> Or some frail *China* Jar receive a Flaw,
> Or stain her Honour, or her new Brocade,
> Forget her Pray'rs, or miss a Masquerade,
> Or lose her Heart, or Necklace, at a Ball;
> Or whether Heav'n has doom'd that *Shock* must fall.

But the chief excellence of the satire afforded by the additions consists in the way they mock human and literary matters simultaneously. This is obvious in small ways and in large. Pope cannot arrange for the sylphs to affect the central action of a poem which was complete without them. He therefore makes them desire to affect it and only be prevented from doing so by forces within the poem itself. It is Belinda herself who renders them powerless. She has been warned by her would-be protector, Ariel, that trouble is ahead, but his help is impotent when she transgresses the very condition which gives him power:

> Just in that instant, anxious *Ariel* sought
> The close Recesses of the Virgin's Thought;
> As on the Nosegay in her Breast reclin'd,
> He watch'd th' Ideas rising in her Mind,
> Sudden he view'd, in spite of all her Art,
> An Earthly Lover lurking at her Heart.
> Amaz'd, confus'd, he found his Pow'r expir'd,
> Resign'd to Fate, and with a Sigh retir'd.

Pope was well pleased with the additions and the way they were made to 'fit so well' with their context. It may, however, be argued that the poem in its 1712 form was better proportioned as a narrative, that the additions are too bulky for the slight thread of the story. Shock, we remember, thought that Belinda, dreaming of Ariel, had slept too long. On the other hand, we could say that the embroidery is spread so thickly that the tenuous net on which it is loaded is kept firmly in place. The reader must judge for himself, remembering that no judgement counts which is not founded on many readings of the later version. The first version is soon assimilated, but the second rewards each successive reading more richly.

NOTE ON THE TEXT

The text of the poem in its five-canto form is that of the first edition corrected in accordance with Pope's revisions: the text of the poem in its two-canto form is that of the first and only edition; except that both versions have been very slightly modernized in order, e.g., to assert the distinction between *ere* and *e'er*; and that a few misprints have been corrected.

KEY TO THE NOTES

Croker:	Notes by J. W. Croker included in Elwin and Courthope's edition of Pope's works (1871–1889)
EC:	Note by Elwin in the edition named above.
Gabalis:	The Count of Gabalis, by Abbé de Villars, translated by P. Ayres. 1680
Holden:	The Rape of the Lock, edited by G. Holden. 1909
Iliad:	Homer's *Iliad*, translated by Pope. 1715–20
Johnson:	Johnson's Dictionary. 1755. In most of the instances where his definition is quoted, Johnson quotes the line in question as one of his examples
Odyssey:	Homer's *Odyssey*, translated by Pope. 1725
OED:	The Oxford English Dictionary. 1884–1928
P:	A note by Pope. His notes are here printed in italics

Phillips, E.: The New World of English Words. Edition of 1706

Wakefield: Works of A. Pope. Edited by G. Wakefield. 1794. Observations on Pope, by G. Wakefield. 1796.

Warburton: Works of A. Pope. Edited by W. Warburton. 1751

Warton: An Essay on the Genius and Writings of Pope. Edition of 1806. Works of A. Pope. Edited by J. Warton. 1797

THE RAPE OF THE LOCK
AN HEROI-COMICAL POEM
IN FIVE CANTO'S

Nolueram, Belinda, tuos violare capillos,
Sed juvat hoc precibus me tribuisse tuis.

MARTIAL.

TO
MRS ARABELLA FERMOR

MADAM,

It will be in vain to deny that I have some Regard for
this Piece, since I Dedicate it to You. Yet You may bear
me Witness, it was intended only to divert a few young
Ladies, who have good Sense and good Humour enough,
to laugh not only at their Sex's little unguarded Follies,   5
but at their own. But as it was communicated with the
Air of a Secret, it soon found its Way into the World.

Pope substitutes 'Belinda' for Martial's 'Polytime': the motto may be
translated: 'I was loth, Belinda, to violate your locks; but I am pleased to
have granted that much to your prayers.'

Mrs.] the title of a lady whether married or single. *Arabella Fermor*]
See Introduction. Arabella Fermor was the daughter of Henry Fermor of
Tusmore and Somerton, Oxon., and of Ellen, second daughter and co-heir
of Sir George Browne of Wickhambreux, Kent. The date of her birth is
unknown, but probably fell between 1688 and 1690. On 25 March 1693
we find her arriving at the English Convent in Paris, where she stayed nine
years, absenting herself for considerable periods in order to 'perfect her
French' in other houses. She returned to England in 1704, and four years
later began to be celebrated by the poets as a 'beauty'. Late in 1714 or early
in 1715 she married Francis Perkins of Ufton Court, Berks. There were
six children of the marriage. She died in 1738, two years after her husband.
1 ff. This dedication is written in the manner of the polite correspondence
of the time which modelled itself on that of French writers of the seven-
teenth century, notable among whom was Voiture. The letter which
Belinda receives at i. 118 f. belongs to an older fashion.
4–9 *good Sense and good Humour . . . Good-Nature*] See note on v. 16, 30 f.below.

An imperfect Copy having been offer'd to a Bookseller, You had the Good-Nature for my Sake to consent to the Publication of one more correct: This I was forc'd   10 to before I had executed half my Design, for the *Machinery* was entirely wanting to compleat it.

The *Machinery*, Madam, is a Term invented by the Criticks, to signify that Part which the Deities, Angels, or Dæmons, are made to act in a Poem: for the ancient   15 Poets are in one respect like many modern Ladies; Let an Action be never so trivial in it self, they always make it appear of the utmost Importance. These Machines I determin'd to raise on a very new and odd Foundation, the *Rosicrucian* Doctrine of Spirits.   20

I know how disagreeable it is to make use of hard Words before a Lady; but 'tis so much the Concern of a Poet to have his Works understood, and particularly by your Sex, that You must give me leave to explain two or three difficult Terms.   25

The *Rosicrucians* are a People I must bring You acquainted with. The best Account I know of them is in a French Book call'd *Le Comte de Gabalis*, which both in its Title and Size is so like a *Novel*, that many of the Fair Sex have read it for one by Mistake. According to   30 these Gentlemen, the four Elements are inhabited by *Salamanders*. The *Gnomes*, or Dæmons of Earth, delight

20 f. *Rosicrucian Doctrine*] See Appendix B, pp. 93 ff. below.

29 *Title and Size*] *The Count de Soissons* and *The Count of Amboise* are two of the novels translated from the French and included in the series of 'Modern Novels' (published by Richard Bentley) in which Ayres's translation of *Gabalis* appeared. The size of them all is duodecimo.

32 *Gnomes*] In *Gabalis* these, like all the other spirits, are 'good', but, living in the earth near to the Devil, they have been frightened into helping

Spirits, which they call *Sylphs*, *Gnomes*, *Nymphs*, and in Mischief; but the *Sylphs*, whose Habitation is in the Air, are the best-condition'd Creatures imaginable. For they say, any Mortals may enjoy the most intimate Familiarities with these gentle Spirits, upon a Condition very easie to all true *Adepts*, an inviolate Preservation of Chastity.

As to the following Canto's, all the Passages of them are as Fabulous, as the Vision at the Beginning, or the Transformation at the End; (except the Loss of your Hair, which I always mention with Reverence). The Human Persons are as Fictitious as the Airy ones; and the Character of *Belinda*, as it is now manag'd, resembles You in nothing but in Beauty.

If this Poem had as many Graces as there are in Your Person, or in Your Mind, yet I could never hope it should pass thro' the World half so Uncensured as You have done. But let its Fortune be what it will, mine is happy enough, to have given me this Occasion of assuring You that I am, with the truest Esteem,

Madam,

Your Most Obedient Humble Servant.

A. POPE.

---

him to make 'the Soul of a man become Mortal'. Pope makes them mischievous by nature.

39 *Chastity*] The renunciation of 'all Carnal Commerce with Women' is, according to *Gabalis*, the first condition for men who wish to control the sylphs. Unless the sylphs could gain an earthly lover, they never achieved immortality.

45 *Belinda*] A fashionable name of the time, being that, e.g., of a 'gentle-woman' in Etherege's *Man of Mode*, and of an 'affected lady' in Congreve's *Old Bachelor*. It was especially appropriate for one who was known to her friends as Belle Fermor.

CANTO I

What dire Offence from am'rous Causes springs,
What mighty Contests rise from trivial Things,
I sing – This Verse to *Caryll*, Muse! is due;
This, ev'n *Belinda* may vouchsafe to view:
Slight is the Subject, but not so the Praise   5
If She inspire, and He approve my Lays.

The first sketch of this Poem was written in less than a fortnight's time, in 1711, in two Canto's, and so printed in a Miscellany, without the name of the Author. The Machines were not inserted till a year after, when he publish'd it, and annex'd the foregoing Dedication. (P)

1–12 Cowley, in one of the notes to his epic *Davideis*, alleges that 'The custom of beginning all *Poems*, with a *Proposition* of the whole work, and an *Invocation* of some God for his assistance to go through with it, is so solemnly and religiously observed by all the ancient *Poets*, that though I could have found out a better way, I should not (I think) have ventured upon it'.

Wakefield noted the 'concourse of heavy and hissing *consonants*' in the latter half of l. 1; Tennyson considered its sibilants 'horrible'.

3 John Caryll (1666?–1736) was the son of Richard Caryll of West Grinstead, Sussex, and nephew of John Caryll (1625–1711), poet, playwright, English agent at Rome, and secretary to Mary, queen of James II. His uncle's estate at West Harting was forfeited by the Crown following the discovery of complicity in the assassination plot of 1696, life interest in it being granted to Lord Cutts. John Caryll, the nephew, redeemed it in the same year at the price of £6000. Four years later, on his father's death, he came into the property at West Grinstead. Pope had known Caryll at least as early as 1709, and he became his longest correspondent, their letters running from 1711 to 1735. He befriended Gay as well as Pope. Pope may have owed to him his introduction to Steele who had been Lord Cutts's secretary during the negotiations of 1696.

5 Cf. Virgil, *Georgics*, iv, 6 f.:

> In tenui labor; at tenuis non gloria, si quem
> Numina laeva sinunt, auditque vocatus Apollo.

Say what strange Motive, Goddess! cou'd compel
A well-bred *Lord* t'assault a gentle *Belle*?
Oh say what stranger Cause, yet unexplor'd,
Cou'd make a gentle *Belle* reject a *Lord*?   10
In Tasks so bold, can Little Men engage,
And in soft Bosoms dwells such mighty Rage?
  Sol thro' white Curtains shot a tim'rous Ray,
And op'd those Eyes that must eclipse the Day;
Now Lapdogs give themselves the rowzing Shake,   15
And sleepless Lovers, just at Twelve, awake:
Thrice rung the Bell, the Slipper knock'd the Ground,

Sedley's translation had read:

> The Subjects humble, but not so the Praise,
> If any Muse assist the Poets Lays.

And Dryden's:

> Slight is the Subject, but the Praise not small,
> If Heav'n assist, and *Phœbus* hear my Call.

Pope combines the two for l. 5.

11 *Little Men*] Pope is stating the discrepancy beloved of the mock-heroic; he is also referring to Lord Petre's short stature.

12 Cf. *Æneid*, i 11: . . . Tantaene animis caelestibus irae? (Such fierce resentment in heavenly breasts?) which has been described as 'a characteristic touch of the poet's gentle nature: with an undertone of sadness too'. This undertone improves the mockery of Boileau's 'Tant de fiel entre-t-il dans l'âme des dévots?' (*Lutrin*, i 12) and of Pope's echo here.

13 The curtains are those of the four-poster bed.

14 Pope is using the hyperbole of the Elizabethan sonnets; cf. ii 1–4 below.

15 *Lapdogs*] See note on iii 158 below.

17 The triple repetition is common in epic poetry: in Garth's mock-heroic *Dispensary*

> The Sage transported at th' approaching Hour,
> Imperiously thrice thunder'd on the Floor.

'Belinda rung a hand-bell, which not being answered, she knocked with her slipper. Bell-hanging was not introduced into our domestic apartments

And the press'd Watch return'd a silver Sound.
Belinda still her downy Pillow prest,
Her Guardian *Sylph* prolong'd the balmy Rest.   20
'Twas he had summon'd to her silent Bed
The Morning-Dream that hover'd o'er her Head.
A Youth more glitt'ring than a *Birth-night Beau*,
(That ev'n in Slumber caus'd her Cheek to glow)
Seem'd to her Ear his winning Lips to lay,   25
And thus in Whispers said, or seem'd to say.

    Fairest of Mortals, thou distinguish'd Care
Of thousand bright Inhabitants of Air!
If e'er one Vision touch'd thy infant Thought,

---

till long after [this] date. I myself, about the year 1790, remember that it was still the practice for ladies to summon their attendants to their bed-chambers by knocking with a high-heeled shoe' (Croker).

18 By 1700 London watches were held to be the best in the world. The first repeaters sounded the hour and the quarters when a string was pulled. Belinda's watch was of a more advanced design which struck when pressure was applied to the pendant. The chime—so many for the hour and then 2, 4, or 6 for the quarter just passed—came from a bell screwed into the back of the case. The difficulty of striking a light made repeaters popular.

20 There is no inconsistency, as Croker thought, between ll. 14 and 20. Belinda opens her eyes at l. 14. It is noon but the curtains shut out the full light. (The light is 'tim'rous' because of the curtains, and because of the sacredness of Belinda's bedroom.) She has fallen asleep again by l. 19.

21 ff. The gods sometimes communicate with the epic hero by means of apparitions during sleep. Ariel summons a dream in which he figures in a disguise calculated to interest Belinda. His calculation succeeds (see l. 24). His normal appearance is described at ii 70 ff.

23 The dresses worn for the royal birthday celebrations were exceptionally splendid.

26 *said, or seem'd to say*] Pope is echoing Virgil, *Æneid*, vi 454, and *Paradise Lost*, i 781 ff.

Of all the Nurse and all the Priest have taught,   30
Of airy Elves by Moonlight Shadows seen,
The silver Token, and the circled Green,
Or Virgins visited by Angel-Pow'rs,
With Golden Crowns and Wreaths of heav'nly Flow'rs,
Hear and believe! thy own Importance know,   35
Nor bound thy narrow Views to Things below.
Some secret Truths from Learned Pride conceal'd,
To Maids alone and Children are reveal'd:
What tho' no Credit doubting Wits may give?
The Fair and Innocent shall still believe.   40
Know then, unnumber'd Spirits round thee fly,
The light *Militia* of the lower Sky;
These, tho' unseen, are ever on the Wing,
Hang o'er the *Box*, and hover round the *Ring*.

30–4 The nurse and the priest were considered by seventeenth-century philosophers and educationalists as the chief inlets of superstition: cf. Dryden, *Hind and Panther*, iii 389 ff.:

> By education most have been misled . . .
> The *Priest* continues what the nurse began;

The nurse's lore is that of ll. 31 f., the priest's that of ll. 33 f.
32 Fairies were supposed to leave a silver coin in the slipper of dutiful maid-servants. For fairy rings see Dryden, *Wife of Bath Her Tale*, 1–23.
33 Carrying a reference to the Annunciation and to the experiences of virgin saints.
37 f. Cf. St Matthew, xi 25.
41 *lower Sky*] The militia is composed of aerial sylphs as distinct from ethereal.
44 Cf. the Earl of Dorset, *On the Countess of Dorchester . . . Written in 1680*, 6 f.:

> Wilt thou still sparkle in the box,
> Still ogle in the ring.

The open-air pleasures of the Restoration court were mainly those of promenading the Mall in St James's Park, and of driving round the Ring

Think what an Equipage thou hast in Air,   45
And view with scorn *Two Pages* and a *Chair*.
As now your own, our Beings were of old,
And once inclos'd in Woman's beauteous Mold;
Thence, by a soft Transition, we repair
From earthly Vehicles to these of Air.   50
Think not, when Woman's transient Breath is fled,
That all her Vanities at once are dead:
Succeeding Vanities she still regards,
And tho' she plays no more, o'erlooks the Cards.
Her Joy in gilded Chariots, when alive,   55

(called also the Tour or Circus) in Hyde Park. The Ring was north of the eastern end of what is now the Serpentine, and being on high ground had views of open country on almost all sides. It measured two or three hundred yards in diameter. A foreigner observed that 'the coaches drive slowly round, some in one direction, others in the opposite way, which . . . produces a rather pretty effect, and proves clearly that they only come there in order to see and to be seen'. Even during William's reign, when it was supposed to suffer from the general decline of gaiety, a French observer noted that he had 'often computed near 500 Coaches, that vie one with another for splendor and equipage'. Under Anne its popularity again increased. By 1736 it had ceased to be fashionable. The road north of Rotten Row is still called 'Ring Road'. See note on iv 117 below.

45 *Equipage*] = A carriage and horses, with attendant footmen. Their extravagance had been censured in *Tatler* 144, and *Spectator* 15.

46 *a Chair*] a sedan chair.

47 ff. The origin of this system of soul-transmigration is Ovid's *Metamorphoses*, xv.

50 *Vehicles*] 'The *Platonists* doe chiefly take notice of *Three* Kindes of *Vehicles*, *Æthereal*, *Aereal*, and *Terrestrial*' (Henry More, *Immortality of the Soul*). Pope intends a pun linking vehicles and equipages.

55 f.   – *Quæ gratia currûm*
            Armorumque fuit vivis, quæ cura nitentes
            Pascere equos, eadem sequitur repostos.

And Love of *Ombre*, after Death survive.
For when the Fair in all their Pride expire,
To their first Elements their Souls retire:
The Sprights of fiery Termagants in Flame
Mount up, and take a *Salamander's* Name.   60
Soft yielding Minds to Water glide away,
And sip with *Nymphs*, their Elemental Tea.
The graver Prude sinks downward to a *Gnome*,
In search of Mischief still on Earth to roam.
The light Coquettes in *Sylphs* aloft repair,   65
And sport and flutter in the Fields of Air.

   Know farther yet; Whoever fair and chaste
Rejects Mankind, is by some *Sylph* embrac'd:
For Spirits, freed from mortal Laws, with ease
Assume what Sexes and what Shapes they please.   70
What guards the Purity of melting Maids,
In Courtly Balls, and Midnight Masquerades,

Virgil, *Æneid* 6. (P) Dryden's translation (vi 890 f.) ran:

        The love of Horses which they had, alive,
        And care of Chariots, after Death survive.

   The carriages of the time were called 'chariots': Pope intends a pun, satirizing contemporary society under cover of epic quotation.

Ombre] See iii 27 ff. below.

58 *first*] = preponderating. A person's nature was supposed to depend on the relative proportions of the four elements in the composition of his body.

59 'Termagant . . . A scold; a brawling turbulent woman' (Johnson).

61 Cf. the transformation of Proteus, Virgil, *Georgics*, iv 410: 'aut in aquas tenuis dilapsus abibit' (or he will melt into fleeting water and be gone).

62 *Tea*] Then a perfect rhyme with *away*. Cf. iii 7 f. below.

66 *Fields of Air*] Cf. *Æneid*, vi 888: 'Aeris in campis latis'.

69 ff. Cf. *Paradise Lost*, i 423 ff.

72 *Midnight Masquerades*] *Spectator* 8 is up in arms against these masked balls.

B

Safe from the treach'rous Friend, the daring Spark,
The Glance by Day, the Whisper in the Dark;
When kind Occasion prompts their warm Desires,   75
When Musick softens, and when Dancing fires?
'Tis but their *Sylph*, the wise Celestials know,
Tho' *Honour* is the Word with Men below.

   Some Nymphs there are, too conscious of their Face,
For Life predestin'd to the *Gnomes*' Embrace.   80
These swell their Prospects and exalt their Pride,
When Offers are disdain'd, and Love deny'd.
Then gay Ideas crowd the vacant Brain;
While Peers and Dukes, and all their sweeping Train,
And Garters, Stars, and Coronets appear,   85
And in soft Sounds, *Your Grace* salutes their Ear.
'Tis these that early taint the Female Soul,
Instruct the Eyes of young *Coquettes* to roll,
Teach Infant-Cheeks a bidden Blush to know,
And little Hearts to flutter at a *Beau*.   90

   Oft when the World imagine Women stray,
The *Sylphs* thro' mystick Mazes guide their Way,
Thro' all the giddy Circle they pursue,
And old Impertinence expel by new.

---

73 *Spark*] 'A lively, showy, splendid, gay man. It is commonly used in contempt' (Johnson).

77 f. Cf. Dryden, *Hind and the Panther*, iii 823 f.:

> Immortal pow'rs the term of conscience know,
> But int'rest is her name with men below.

79 *too . . . Face*] who think too much of their looks.

88 *Spectator* 46 presents an Ogling-Master who sets up to teach 'the whole Art of Ogling'.

89 i.e., with rouge.

94 *Impertinence*] 'Trifle: thing of no value' (Johnson).

What tender Maid but must a Victim fall   95
To one Man's Treat, but for another's Ball?
When *Florio* speaks, what Virgin could withstand,
If gentle *Damon* did not squeeze her Hand?
With varying Vanities, from ev'ry Part,
They shift the moving Toyshop of their Heart;   100
Where Wigs with Wigs, with Sword-knots Sword-
        knots strive,
Beaus banish Beaus, and Coaches Coaches drive.
This erring Mortals Levity may call,
Oh blind to Truth! the *Sylphs* contrive it all.

    Of these am I, who thy Protection claim,   105
A watchful Sprite, and *Ariel* is my Name.
Late, as I rang'd the Crystal Wilds of Air,
In the clear Mirror of thy ruling *Star*
I saw, alas! some dread Event impend,

96 *Treat*] An entertainment of food and drink.
99 ff. Cf. *Guardian*, 106: 'As I cast my Eye upon her Bosom, it appeared
to be all of Chrystal, and so wonderfully transparent, that I saw every
Thought in her Heart. The first Images I discovered in it were Fans, Silks,
Ribbonds, Laces, and many other Gewgaws, which lay so thick together,
that the whole Heart was nothing else but a Toy-shop. These all faded
away and vanished, when immediately I discerned a long Train of Coaches
and six, Equipages and Liveries that ran through the Heart one after
another in a very great hurry [and so on to cards, a play-house, a church,
a court, a lap-dog, etc.].'
101 f. Cf. *Iliad*, iv 508 f.:

            Now Shield with Shield, with Helmet Helmet clos'd,
        To Armour Armour, Lance to Lance oppos'd.

    Sword-knots] 'Ribband tied to the hilt of the sword' (Johnson).
105 *thy Protection*] = my protection of thee.
107 ff. Cf. the speeches of Uriel and Gabriel, *Paradise Lost*, iv 561 ff.
108 *In the clear Mirror*] *The Language of the Platonists, the writers of the
intelligible world of Spirits, etc.* (P)

Ere to the Main this Morning Sun descend.   110
But Heav'n reveals not what, on how, or where:
Warn'd by thy *Sylph*, oh Pious Maid beware!
This to disclose is all thy Guardian can.
Beware of all, but most beware of Man!

He said; when *Shock*, who thought she slept too long, 115
Leapt up, and wak'd his Mistress with his Tongue.
'Twas then *Belinda*! if Report say true,
Thy Eyes first open'd on a *Billet-doux*;
Wounds, *Charms*, and *Ardors*, were no sooner read,
But all the Vision vanish'd from thy Head.   120

And now, unveil'd, the *Toilet* stands display'd,
Each Silver Vase in mystic Order laid.
First, rob'd in White, the Nymph intent adores
With Head uncover'd, the *Cosmetic* Pow'rs.
A heav'nly Image in the Glass appears,   125
To that she bends, to that her Eyes she rears;
Th'inferior Priestess, at her Altar's side,
Trembling, begins the sacred Rites of Pride.

---

115 The shock or shough was a kind of lap-dog thought to have been brought to England from Iceland. A description printed in 1688 runs: 'an Island Dog . . . of a pretty bigness: curled and rough all over, which by the reason of the length of their hair, make shew neither of face, nor of body: these Curs are much set by, with Ladys, who usually wash, comb, and trim of all the hair of their hinder parts, leaving only the fore parts, and hinder feet jagged'.

118 Belinda's eyes had opened before (l. 14) but had closed again during the morning dream. They now re-open and see the billet-doux, the first (if the report say true) that she had ever received. Report was, of course, lying: see l. 138 below.

119 See note on dedicatory epistle, ll. 1 ff., p. 25 above.

123 ff. Belinda adores her 'heav'nly Image' in the mirror; her image is the 'Goddess', she is the chief priestess.

Unnumber'd Treasures ope at once, and here
The various Off'rings of the World appear;   130
From each she nicely culls with curious Toil,
And decks the Goddess with the glitt'ring Spoil.
This Casket *India's* glowing Gems unlocks,
And all *Arabia* breathes from yonder Box.
The Tortoise here and Elephant unite,   135
Transform'd to *Combs*, the speckled and the white,
Here Files of Pins extend their shining Rows,
Puffs, Powders, Patches, Bibles, Billet-doux.
Now awful Beauty puts on all its Arms;
The Fair each moment rises in her Charms,   140
Repairs her Smiles, awakens ev'ry Grace
And calls forth all the Wonders of her Face;

132 *glitt'ring Spoil*] This, in the plural, is the phase for captive armour in Dryden's *Æneid*, ix 495.

135 f. A small Ovidian metamorphosis.

137 f. The rhyme is imperfect; cf. i 117 f. above.

138 A parody, with a difference, of *Paradise Lost*, ii 621:

> Rocks, Caves, Lakes, Fens, Bogs, Dens, and shades of death.

138 Wakefield compares Charles Montagu, Earl of Halifax (*Supplement to the Works of the Most celebrated Minor Poets*, 1750, p. 46):

> Her waiting-maids prevent the peep of day,
> And, all in order, on her toilet lay
> Prayer-book, patch-boxes, sermon-notes and paint,
> At once t'improve the sinner and the saint.

139 ff. Pope is parodying the arming of the epic hero. The motto of the passage might be that of Keats' *Hyperion*, ii 228 f.:

> . . . for 'tis the eternal law
> That first in beauty should be first in might.

140 Cf. 'the swelling and growing figures of the poets: of which *Fame*, the *Sibyl*, and the *Pestilence* of *Virgil*, with the *Satan* of *Milton*, are sublime examples' (Wakefield).

Sees by Degrees a purer Blush arise,
And keener Lightnings quicken in her Eyes.
The busy *Sylphs* surround their darling Care;   145
These set the Head, and those divide the Hair,
Some fold the Sleeve, while others plait the Gown;
And *Betty's* prais'd for Labours not her own.

CANTO II

Not with more Glories, in th' Etherial Plain,
The Sun first rises o'er the purpled Main,
Than issuing forth, the Rival of his Beams
Lanch'd on the Bosom of the Silver *Thames.*
Fair Nymphs, and well-drest Youths around her shone,   5
But ev'ry Eye was fix'd on her alone.
On her white Breast a sparkling *Cross* she wore,
Which *Jews* might kiss, and Infidels adore.
Her lively Looks a sprightly Mind disclose,
Quick as her Eyes, and as unfix'd as those: 10
Favours to none, to all she Smiles extends,
Oft she rejects, but never once offends.
Bright as the Sun, her Eyes the Gazers strike,

144 Belinda employs the juice of belladonna (deadly nightshade) to enlarge the pupils of the eye, or darkens the surrounding skin.

145 *Antient Traditions of the Rabbi's relate, that several of the fallen Angels became amorous of Women, and particularize some; among the rest* Asael, *who lay with* Naamah, *the wife of* Noah, *or of* Ham; *and who continuing impenitent, still presides over the Women's Toilets.* Bereshi Rabbi *in* Genes. 6. 2. (P)

147 plait] 'fold' (Johnson).

148 *Betty*] In Congreve's *Old Bachelor* there is a maid Betty (and 'an affected Lady' Belinda). Betty was used almost as a generic name for a lady's maid.

1 ff. Cf. Æneas's voyage up the Tiber (*Æneid*, vii); and Shadwell's voyage on the Thames, Dryden's *Mac Flecknoe*, 38 ff.

And, like the Sun, they shine on all alike.
Yet graceful Ease, and Sweetness void of Pride,   15
Might hide her Faults, if *Belles* had Faults to hide:
If to her share some Female Errors fall,
Look on her Face, and you'll forget 'em all.

This Nymph, to the Destruction of Mankind,
Nourish'd two Locks, which graceful hung behind   20
In equal Curls, and well conspir'd to deck
With shining Ringlets her smooth Iv'ry Neck.
Love in these Labyrinths his Slaves detains,
And mighty Hearts are held in slender Chains.
With hairy Sprindges we the Birds betray,   25
Slight Lines of Hair surprize the Finny Prey,
Fair Tresses Man's Imperial Race insnare,
And Beauty draws us with a single Hair.

Th' Adventurous *Baron* the bright Locks admir'd,

15 *Ease*] Considered as the test of good breeding.
25 *Sprindges*] Traps.
29 ff. Pope mimics *Æneid*, xi, where Camilla, seeking to attack Chloreus,
is tracked down by Arruns. Dryden's translation (ll. 1101 ff.) reads:

> Then, *Aruns* doom'd to Death, his Arts assay'd
> To Murther, unespy'd, the *Volscian* Maid. . . .
> He threats, and trembles, trying ev'ry Way
> Unseen to kill, and safely to betray.
>   *Chloreus*, the priest of *Cybelè*, from far,
> Glitt'ring in *Phrygian* Arms amidst the War,
> Was by the Virgin view'd . . .
> Him, the fierce Maid beheld with ardent Eyes;
> Fond and Ambitious of so Rich a Prize . . .
> Blind in her haste, she chases him alone,
> And seeks his Life, regardless of her own.
> This lucky Moment the slye Traytor chose:
> Then, starting from his Ambush up he rose, } . . .
> And threw, but first to Heav'n address'd his Vows.

He saw, he wish'd, and to the Prize aspir'd: 30
Resolv'd to win, he meditates the way,
By Force to ravish, or by Fraud betray;
For when Success a Lover's Toil attends,
Few ask, if Fraud or Force attain'd his Ends.

For this, ere *Phœbus* rose, he had implor'd   35
Propitious Heav'n, and ev'ry Pow'r ador'd,
But chiefly *Love* – to *Love* an Altar built,
Of twelve vast *French* Romances, neatly gilt.
There lay three Garters, half a Pair of Gloves;
And all the Trophies of his former Loves.   40
With tender *Billet-doux* he lights the Pyre,
And breathes three am'rous Sighs to raise the Fire.
Then prostrate falls, and begs with ardent Eyes
Soon to obtain, and long possess the Prize:
The Pow'rs gave Ear, and granted half his Pray'r,   45
The rest, the Winds dispers'd in empty Air.

But now secure the painted Vessel glides,
The Sun-beams trembling on the floating Tydes,
While melting Musick steals upon the Sky,
And soften'd Sounds along the Waters die.   50

'Give me, propitious Pow'r, to wash away
The Stains of this dishonourable Day . . .
Let me, by stealth, this Female Plague o'ercome;
And from the Field, return inglorious home.'
    Apollo heard, and granting half his Pray'r,
Shuffled in Winds the rest, and toss'd in empty Air.

31 *meditates*] plans.
34 Cf. *Æneid*, ii 390: 'dolus, an virtus, quis in hoste requirat?' (whether deceit or valour, who would ask in warfare?).
38 The protracted heroic romances written in France in the seventeenth century, which were still fashionable.
47 *secure*] free from care (Latin, *securus*).

Smooth flow the Waves, the Zephyrs gently play,
Belinda smil'd, and all the World was gay.
All but the *Sylph* – With careful Thoughts opprest,
Th'impending Woe sate heavy on his Breast.
He summons strait his Denizens of Air;   55
The lucid Squadrons round the Sails repair:
Soft o'er the Shrouds Aerial Whispers breathe,
That seem'd but *Zephyrs* to the Train beneath.
Some to the Sun their Insect-Wings unfold,
Waft on the Breeze, or sink in Clouds of Gold.   60
Transparent Forms, too fine for mortal Sight,
Their fluid Bodies half dissolv'd in Light.
Loose to the Wind their airy Garments flew,
Thin glitt'ring Textures of the filmy Dew;
Dipt in the richest Tincture of the Skies,   65
Where Light disports in ever-mingling Dies,
While ev'ry Beam new transient Colours flings,
Colours that change whene'er they wave their Wings.
Amid the Circle, on the gilded Mast,

53 f. Cf. Dryden, *Æneid*, iv i:

>   But anxious Cares already seiz'd the Queen;

and *Iliad*, x i ff.:

>   All Night the Chiefs before their Vessels lay,
>   And lost in Sleep the Labours of the Day:
>   All but the King; with various Thoughts opprest,
>   His Country's Cares lay rowling in his Breast;

55 *Denizens*] Used in its proper sense of 'naturalized aliens'.
56 ff. See Appendix B, p. 95 below.
64 The gossamer, spun in autumn by a kind of spider that sails through the air, was formerly supposed to be the product of sun-burnt dew.
65 In *Gabalis* the sylphs are 'cloathed in divers Colours'; cf. also *Paradise Lost*, v 283 ff., 'colours dipt in Heav'n . . . skie-tinctur'd grain'.

Superior by the Head, was *Ariel* plac'd;   70
His Purple Pinions opening to the Sun,
He rais'd his Azure Wand, and thus begun.

 Ye *Sylphs* and *Sylphids*, to your Chief give Ear,
Fays, *Fairies*, *Genii*, *Elves*, and *Dæmons* hear!
Ye know the Spheres and various Tasks assign'd,   75
By Laws Eternal, to th' Aerial Kind.
Some in the Fields of purest *Æther* play,
And bask and whiten in the Blaze of Day.
Some guide the Course of wandring Orbs on high,
Or roll the Planets thro' the boundless Sky.   80
Some less refin'd, beneath the Moon's pale Light
Pursue the Stars that shoot athwart the Night,
Or suck the Mists in grosser Air below,
Or dip their Pinions in the painted Bow,
Or brew fierce Tempests on the wintry Main,   85
Or o'er the Glebe distill the kindly Rain.

70 The hero in epic is always taller than his followers.

72 *azure*] Ariel demands a sky-coloured wand.

 begun] In Pope's time the preterite as well as the past participle.

73 *Sylphids*] The female sylph in *Gabalis* is called a *sylphide*.

74 With the exception of 'Elves' (cf. i 31 above) all these names are found in *Gabalis*. Pope is finding difficulty in parodying *Paradise Lost*, v 601:

 Thrones, Dominations, Princedomes, Vertues, Powers.

75 ff. *Sphere* is here used in the sense of 'province; compass of knowledge or action' (Johnson). In *Gabalis* each sylph, etc., has control of the element he inhabits; 'they trouble the *Air*, and the *Sea*, set the Earth in Combustion, and dispense the Fire of *Heaven*, according to their Humour'.

77 ff. This division of occupation is in the epic style: cf. *Æneid*, vi 642 ff., and *Paradise Lost*, ii 528 ff.

79 See Appendix B, p. 96 below.

82 Until the edition of 1736 this line read:

 Hover, and catch the shooting Stars by Night,

Others on Earth o'er human Race preside,
Watch all their Ways, and all their Actions guide:
Of these the Chief the Care of Nations own,
And guard with Arms Divine the *British Throne*.   90
   Our humbler Province is to tend the Fair,
Not a less pleasing, tho' less glorious Care.
To save the Powder from too rude a Gale,
Nor let th' imprison'd Essences exhale,
To draw fresh Colours from the vernal Flow'rs,   95
To steal from Rainbows ere they drop in Show'rs
A brighter Wash; to curl their waving Hairs,
Assist their Blushes, and inspire their Airs;
Nay oft, in Dreams, Invention we bestow,
To change a *Flounce*, or add a *Furbelo*.   100
   This Day, black Omens threat the brightest Fair
That e'er deserv'd a watchful Spirit's Care;
Some dire Disaster, or by Force, or Slight,
But what, or where, the Fates have wrapt in Night.
Whether the Nymph shall break *Diana*'s Law,   105
Or some frail *China* Jar receive a Flaw,
Or stain her Honour, or her new Brocade,
Forget her Pray'rs, or miss a Masquerade,
Or lose her Heart, or Necklace, at a Ball;
Or whether Heav'n has doom'd that *Shock* must fall.   110
Haste then ye Spirits! to your Charge repair;

90 Cf. the angel in Addison's *Rosamond*, III i 5 f.

> In hours of peace, unseen, unknown,
> I hover o'er the *British* throne.

97 *Wash*] 'A medical or cosmetick lotion' (Johnson).
100 *Furbelo*] 'A piece of stuff plaited and puckered together, either below or above, on the petticoats or gowns of women' (Johnson).
103 *Slight*] Sleight; trick.

The flutt'ring Fan be *Zephyretta*'s Care;
The Drops to thee, *Brillante*, we consign;
And, *Momentilla*, let the Watch be thine;
Do thou, *Crispissa*, tend her fav'rite Lock;   115
Ariel himself shall be the Guard of *Shock*.

  To Fifty chosen *Sylphs*, of special Note,
We trust th'important Charge, the *Petticoat*:
Oft have we known that sev'nfold Fence to fail,
Tho' stiff with Hoops, and arm'd with Ribs of Whale.   120
Form a strong Line about the Silver Bound,
And guard the wide Circumference around.

  Whatever Spirit, careless of his charge,
His Post neglects, or leaves the Fair at large,
Shall feel sharp Vengeance soon o'ertake his Sins,   125
Be stopt in *Vials*, or transfixt with *Pins*;
Or plung'd in Lakes of bitter *Washes* lie,
Or wedg'd whole Ages in a *Bodkin*'s Eye:

113 *Drops*] 'Diamond(s) hanging in the ear' (Johnson).

115 *Crispissa*] 'To crisp in our earlier writers is a common word for curl, from the Latin *crispo*' (Wakefield).

116 The reason for Ariel's special post is hinted at iii 158 and iv 75 f.

117 ff. Pope mimics the epic shield; cf. *Iliad*, xviii 701 ff., where Vulcan, making the shield of Achilles, binds the circumference with silver. 'The hoop petticoat, in spite of the notion of Addison, that "a touch of his pen would make it contract like a sensitive plant" (see *Spectator*, 127), continued in fashion as an ordinary dress for upwards of threescore years' (Croker).

123 ff. Cf. Jove's threats, *Iliad*, viii 11 ff. and 'the various Penances enjoyn'd' before a soul in Hades can be made ready for human life again (*Æneid*, vi 739 ff.).

126 *Vials*] Phials, small bottles.

128 Cf. *Iliad*, v 1090 f., where Mars in imagination sees himself

> . . . pierc'd with *Grecian* Darts, for Ages lie,
> Condemn'd to Pain, tho' fated not to die;

Gums and *Pomatums* shall his Flight restrain,
While clog'd he beats his silken Wings in vain;   130
Or Alom-*Stypticks* with contracting Power
Shrink his thin Essence like a rivell'd Flower.
Or as *Ixion* fix'd, the Wretch shall feel
The giddy Motion of the whirling Mill,
In Fumes of burning Chocolate shall glow,   135
And tremble at the Sea that froaths below!
  He spoke; the Spirits from the Sails descend;
Some, Orb in Orb, around the Nymph extend,
Some thrid the mazy Ringlets of her Hair,
Some hang upon the Pendants of her Ear;   140
With beating Hearts the dire Event they wait,
Anxious, and trembling for the Birth of Fate.

CANTO III

Close by those Meads for ever crown'd with Flow'rs,
Where *Thames* with Pride surveys his rising Tow'rs,
There stands a Structure of Majestick Frame,
Which from the neighb'ring *Hampton* takes its Name.

---

and the fate of Shakespeare's Ariel (*Tempest*, 1 ii 270 ff.). Pope plays on
the various meanings of *bodkin*: (1) here it means a blunt-pointed needle;
(2) at iv 98 and v 95, a hair ornament; (3) at v 55 and 88, a dagger (with
a pun on (2)).

129 *Pomatums*] Ointments.

131 *stypticks*] An astringent, which stops bleeding.

132 *rivell'd*] 'contract[ed] into wrinkles and corrugations' (Johnson).

134 Cf. iii 106 below, and *Iliad*, i 764 (of Vulcan's fall from heaven):

             Breathless I fell, in giddy Motion lost.

138 Cf. the angels in *Paradise Lost*, v 596.

142 Cf. *Iliad*, iv 112: And Fate now labours with some vast Event.

4 'The modern portion of Hampton Court, and the East and South fronts,

Here *Britain*'s Statesmen oft the Fall of foredoom   5
Of Foreign Tyrants, and of Nymphs at home;
Here Thou, Great *Anna*! whom three Realms obey,
Dost sometimes Counsel take – and sometimes *Tea*.

  Hither the Heroes and the Nymphs resort,
To taste awhile the Pleasures of a Court;   10
In various Talk th' instructive hours they past,
Who gave the *Ball*, or paid the *Visit* last:
One speaks the Glory of the *British Queen*,
And one describes a charming *Indian Screen*;
A third interprets Motions, Looks, and Eyes;   15
At ev'ry Word a Reputation dies.
Snuff, or the *Fan*, supply each Pause of Chat,

---

were built by William III, who frequently resided there. Queen Anne only
went there occasionally' (Croker). Holden quotes Hutton's *Hampton Court*:
'[in Anne's reign] it would be difficult to say whether it was better known
as the home of statesmen or the resort of wits'. Hutton explains Anne's
preference for Windsor and Kensington by her connecting Hampton
Court with the death of the Duke of Gloucester (the only child of hers
to survive infancy).

7 The union of England and Wales with Scotland had taken place in 1707.
11 ff. A contemporary description of the Court of King William at
Kensington runs: 'At this Assembly, the only diversion is playing at Cards:
For which purpose there are two Tables for *Basset* and three or four more
for *Picket* and *Ombre*, but generally the Basset-Tables are only fill'd while
the rest of the Company either sit or stand, talking on various Subjects,
or justle about from one end of the Gallery [of pictures] to the other, some
to admire, and most to find fault'.

12 *Visit*] See note on iii 167 below.

17 'The singular growth of the practice of taking snuff was a special feature
of the reign of Queen Anne: before 1702 it was comparatively unknown'
(Holden). An advertisement in *Spectator* 138 undertakes to teach the
exercise of the snuff-box. The programme includes 'Rules for offering
Snuff to a Stranger, a Friend, or a Mistress' and 'The Undertaker does not

With singing, laughing, ogling, and all that.
Mean while declining from the Noon of Day,
The Sun obliquely shoots his burning Ray; 20
The hungry Judges soon the Sentence sign,
And Wretches hang that Jury-men may Dine;
The Merchant from th'*Exchange* returns in Peace,
And the long Labours of the *Toilette* cease –
Belinda now, whom Thirst of Fame invites, 25
Burns to encounter two adventrous Knights,
At *Ombre* singly to decide their Doom;
And swells her Breast with Conquests yet to come.
Strait the three Bands prepare in Arms to join,
Each Band the number of the Sacred Nine. 30
Soon as she spreads her Hand, th' Aerial Guard
Descend, and sit on each important Card:
First *Ariel* perch'd upon a *Matadore*,
Then each, according to the Rank they bore;
For *Sylphs*, yet mindful of their ancient Race, 35

---

question but in a short time to have formed a Body of Regular Snuff-Boxes
ready to meet and make head against all the Regiment of Fans which have
been lately Disciplined, and are now in Motion'. Steele is here referring
back to Addison's paper (102) which had taught the exercise of the fan
under the form of military drill.

29-98 Pope's mock-heroic treatment of the game of Ombre owes some-
thing to Dryden's account of the bees, Virgil's *Georgics*, iv 92 ff.

29 f. Ombre, pronounced *omber*, employs the full pack minus its 8's, 9's
and 10's, and of this forty, each of the three players is dealt nine cards. The
'Sacred Nine' are the Muses: Pope is pretending that the number of cards
dealt to each person has some occult significance.

31 ff. A further example of the sylphs' 'humbler Province' of tending 'the
Fair' (ii 91); cf. i 53 f.

33 The three cards of highest value in ombre are called the Matadores.

34 The Gods in Virgil sit in order.

Are, as when Women, wondrous fond of Place.
   Behold, four *Kings* in Majesty rever'd,
With hoary Whiskers and a forky Beard;
And four fair *Queens* whose hands sustain a Flow'r,
Th' expressive Emblem of their softer Pow'r;   40
Four *Knaves* in Garbs succinct, a trusty Band,
Caps on their heads, and Halberds in their hand;
And Particolour'd Troops, a shining Train,
Draw forth to Combat on the Velvet Plain.
   The skilful Nymph reviews her Force with Care;   45
Let Spades be Trumps! she said, and Trumps they were.
   Now move to War her Sable *Matadores*,
In Show like Leaders of the swarthy *Moors*.
Spadillio first, unconquerable Lord!
Led off two captive Trumps, and swept the Board.   50
As many more *Manillio* forc'd to yield,
And march'd a Victor from the verdant Field.
Him *Basto* follow'd, but his Fate more hard
Gain'd but one Trump and one *Plebeian* Card.

---

37 ff. This review of the forces is epical in all but length. Pope describes accurately the pictures on contemporary cards.

38 *Whiskers*] 'a tuft of Hair on the Upper Lip of a Man' (E. Phillips).

41 *succinct*] girded up; the Knave of the pack was originally a servant, wearing his clothes girded around the waist so that his work would not be impeded.

42 *Halberds*] 'a kind of combination of spear and battle-axe' (OED)

46 Wakefield compares Genesis i 3: 'And God said, "Let there be light:" and there was light', which on the authority of Longinus (*De Sublimitate*, ix) became the most famous of all instances of the sublime.

48 Because Spades are trumps.

49 *Spadillio*] The Ace of Spades.

51 *Manillio*] The 2 of Spades, reckoned the second highest card.

53 *Basto*] The Ace of Clubs, reckoned the third highest card.

With his broad Sabre next, a Chief in Years, 55
The hoary Majesty of *Spades* appears;
Puts forth one manly Leg, to sight reveal'd;
The rest his many-colour'd Robe conceal'd.
The Rebel-*Knave*, who dares his Prince engage,
Proves the just Victim of his Royal Rage. 60
Ev'n mighty *Pam* that Kings and Queens o'erthrew,
And mow'd down Armies in the Fights of *Lu*,
Sad Chance of War! now, destitute of Aid,
Falls undistinguish'd by the Victor *Spade*!

Thus far both Armies to *Belinda* yield; 65
Now to the *Baron* Fate inclines the Field.
His warlike *Amazon* her Host invades,
Th' Imperial Consort of the Crown of *Spades*.
The *Club*'s black Tyrant first her Victim dy'd,
Spite of his haughty Mien, and barb'rous Pride: 70
What boots the Regal Circle on his Head,
His Giant Limbs in State unwieldy spread?
That long behind he trails his pompous Robe,
And of all Monarchs only grasps the Globe?

The *Baron* now his *Diamonds* pours apace; 75
Th'embroider'd *King* who shows but half his Face,
And his refulgent *Queen*, with Pow'rs combin'd,
Of broken Troops, an easie Conquest find.
Clubs, *Diamonds*, *Hearts*, in wild Disorder seen,
With Throngs promiscuous strow the level Green. 80

61 f. Pam, the Knave of Clubs, was 'a sort of paramount trump', taking
precedence even of the ace of the trump suit in the game of Loo or Lu.
71 ff. 'These lines are a parody of several passages in *Virgil*' (Wakefield).
79 Cf. Statius, *Thebaid*, xi 597: 'arma, viri, currus'; and Dryden's *Æneid*,
xi 943:

Arms, Horses, Men, on heaps together lye.

Thus when dispers'd a routed Army runs,
Of *Asia*'s Troops, and *Africk*'s Sable Sons,
With like Confusion different Nations fly,
Of various Habit and of various Dye,
The pierc'd Battalions dis-united fall,   85
In Heaps on Heaps; one Fate o'erwhelms them all.

   The *Knave* of *Diamonds* tries his wily Arts,
And wins (oh shameful Chance!) the *Queen* of *Hearts*.
At this, the Blood the Virgin's Cheek forsook,
A livid Paleness spreads o'er all her Look;   90
She sees, and trembles at th' approaching Ill,
Just in the Jaws of Ruin, and *Codille*.
And now, (as oft in some distemper'd State)
On one nice *Trick* depends the gen'ral Fate.
An *Ace* of Hearts steps forth: The *King* unseen   95
Lurk'd in her Hand, and mourn'd his captive *Queen*.
He springs to Vengeance with an eager pace,
And falls like Thunder on the prostrate *Ace*.
The Nymph exulting fills with Shouts the Sky,
The Walls, the Woods, and long Canals reply.   100

   Oh thoughtless Mortals! ever blind to Fate,
Too soon dejected, and too soon elate!
Sudden these Honours shall be snatch'd away,
And curs'd for ever this Victorious Day.

87 In the 1714 editions the line read:

       The *Knave* of *Diamonds* now exerts his Arts,

92 If either of his opponents won more tricks than the principal player,
the winner was said to give him Codille. Pope is parodying Dryden's
Æneid, vi 384:

       Just in the Gate, and in the Jaws of Hell.

93 *in . . . State*] 'at some critical political juncture' (Holden).
94 *Trick*] in two senses.

For lo! the Board with Cups and Spoons is crown'd,
The Berries crackle, and the Mill turns round.   106
On shining Altars of *Japan* they raise
The silver Lamp; the fiery Spirits blaze.
From silver Spouts the grateful Liquors glide,
While *China*'s Earth receives the smoking Tyde.   110
At once they gratify their Scent and Taste,
And frequent Cups prolong the rich Repast.
Strait hover round the Fair her Airy Band;
Some, as she sip'd, the fuming Liquor fann'd,
Some o'er her Lap their careful Plumes display'd,   115
Trembling, and conscious of the rich Brocade.
Coffee, (which makes the Politician wise,
And see thro' all things with his half-shut Eyes)
Sent up in Vapours to the *Baron*'s Brain
New Stratagems, the radiant Lock to gain.   120
Ah cease rash Youth! desist ere 'tis too late,
Fear the just Gods, and think of *Scylla*'s Fate!

105 ff. Pope's version of the hearty meals in the epic.
106 The berries are first roasted (since they 'crackle') and are then ground.
107 *shining Altars of Japan*] = lacquered tables.
113 ff. More details of the humbler province of the sylphs (see ii 91 above): some are acting as table napkins.
116 Defoe praises the new brocades as 'thick and high'.
117 f. The coffee houses had long been the chief haunt of amateur politicians.
122 ff. *Vide* Ovid, *Metamorphoses*, 8. (P) King Nisus, besieged in Megara by Minos, had a daughter Scylla who, seeing Minos from a watch tower, fell in love with him. The safety of Nisus and his kingdom was known to depend on a purple hair which, among 'those of honourable silver', grew on his head. Scylla plucked out this hair and took it to Minos but met with nothing but abhorrence for her impiety. After his victory he sailed away; whereupon Scylla attempted to cling to his ship till, beaten off by Nisus, who had become an osprey, she also became a bird.

Chang'd to a Bird, and sent to flit in Air,
She dearly pays for *Nisus*' injur'd Hair!

But when to Mischief Mortals bend their Will,   125
How soon they find fit Instruments of Ill!
Just then, *Clarissa* drew with tempting Grace
A two-edg'd Weapon from her shining Case;
So Ladies in Romance assist their Knight,
Present the Spear, and arm him for the Fight.   130
He takes the Gift with rev'rence, and extends
The little Engine on his Fingers' Ends,
This just behind *Belinda*'s Neck he spread,
As o'er the fragrant Steams she bends her Head:
Swift to the Lock a thousand Sprights repair,   135
A thousand Wings, by turns, blow back the Hair,
And thrice they twitch'd the Diamond in her Ear,
Thrice she look'd back, and thrice the Foe drew near.
Just in that instant, anxious *Ariel* sought
The close Recesses of the Virgin's Thought;   140

125 f. Cf. Dryden, *Absalom and Achitophel*, i 79 f.:

> But, when to Sin our byast Nature leans,
> The careful Devil is still at hand with means.

128 *shining Case*] See note on v 116 below.

131 f. Cf. Dryden's *Æneid*, v 543 f. (Dares has taken up the gloves of Entellus thrown down as a challenge):

> Astonish'd at their weight the Heroe stands,
> And poiz'd the pond'rous Engins in his hands.

135 f. A thousand is a number common in epic. Cf. e.g., Rowe, *Part of the Sixth Book of Lucan*:

> A thousand Darts upon his Buckler ring,
> A thousand Jav'lins round his Temples sing.

139 ff. Cf. in the *Iliad* and *Æneid* the way Apollo leaves Hector and Juturna Turnus.

As on the Nosegay in her Breast reclin'd,
He watch'd th' Ideas rising in her Mind,
Sudden he view'd, in spite of all her Art,
An Earthly Lover lurking at her Heart.
Amaz'd, confus'd, he found his Pow'r expir'd,   145
Resigned to Fate, and with a Sigh retir'd.

The Peer now spreads the glitt'ring *Forfex* wide,
T'inclose the Lock; now joins it, to divide.
Ev'n then, before the fatal Engine clos'd,
A wretched *Sylph* too fondly interpos'd;   150
Fate urg'd the Shears, and cut the *Sylph* in twain,
(But Airy Substance soon unites again)
The meeting Points the sacred Hair dissever
From the fair Head, for ever and for ever!

Then flash'd the living Lightning from her Eyes,   155
And Screams of Horror rend th' affrighted Skies
Not louder Shrieks to pitying Heav'n are cast,

144 *Earthly Lover*] See dedicatory epistle, ll. 35 f.
149 f. The sylph is trying to imitate the angel in Cowley's *Davideis* who
puts by the spear which Saul flings at David.
149 The wooden horse is called 'the fatal Engine' in Dryden's *Æneid*, ii 345.
152 *See* Milton, *lib.* 6: *of* Satan *cut asunder by the Angel* Michael. (P)
154 *for ever and for ever!*] 'To emphasise the fact that the hair could not
unite again, as the bisected sylph had done' (Holden). This may be part of
its significance now, but Pope cannot have so intended it from the start
since sylphs do not appear in the first version.
155 Lightnings break forth from the eyes of the angry Saul in Cowley's
Davideis.
157 ff. A common device in epic. Cf., e.g., *Iliad*, xiv 456 ff.:

> Both Armies join: Earth thunders, Ocean roars.
> Not half so loud the bellowing Deeps resound,
> When stormy Winds disclose the dark Profound;
> Less loud the Winds, that from th' *Æolian* Hall
> Roar thro the Woods, and make whole Forests fall.

When Husbands or when Lap–dogs breathe their last,
Or when rich *China* Vessels, fal'n from high,
In glittring Dust and painted Fragments lie!   160
   Let Wreaths of Triumph now my Temples twine,
(The Victor cry'd) the glorious Prize is mine!
While Fish in Streams, or Birds delight in Air,
Or in a Coach and Six the *British* Fair,
As long as *Atalantis* shall be read,   165

158 In the 1712 edition Pope had '*Lap–dogs*' (i 122); in the 1714 editions
'Monkeys'; and in 1717 he reverted to '*Lap–dogs*'. *Tatler* 47 reports that
'The disconsolate *Maria* has three Days kept her Chamber for the Loss of
the beauteous *Fidelia*, her Lap–dog'; and cf. *Tatler* 121: 'when [the fair
sex] have disappointed themselves of the proper Objects of Love, as Hus-
bands, or Children, such Virgins have exactly at such a Year, grown fond
of Lap-Dogs, Parrats, or other Animals.'

163 ff. Warburton compares Virgil, *Eclogues*, v 76 f.:

> Dum iuga montis aper, fluvios dum pisces amabit,
> Dumque thymo pascentur apes, dum rore cicadæ,
> Semper honos nomenque tuum laudesque manebunt,

which Dryden had translated:

> While savage Boars delight in shady Woods,
> And finny Fish inhabit in the Floods;
> While Bees on Thime, and Locusts feed on Dew,
> Thy grateful Swains these Honours shall renew.

Pope had a more apposite epic source in Dryden's *Æneid*, i 854 ff.
(Æneas' speech to Dido, pleading for hospitality):

> While rowling Rivers into Seas shall run,
> And round the space of Heav'n the radiant Sun;
> While Trees the Mountain tops with Shades supply,
> Your Honour, Name, and Praise shall never dye.

164 No equipage in the Ring was complete without its six grey Flanders
mares and its coat of arms emblazoned on the panels.

165 Mrs Manley's *Secret Memoirs and Manners of several Persons of Quality,
of Both Sexes. From the New Atalantis, an Island in the Mediteranean*, had

Or the small Pillow grace a Lady's Bed,
While *Visits* shall be paid on solemn Days,
When numerous Wax-lights in bright Order blaze,
While Nymphs take Treats, or Assignations give,
So long my Honour, Name, and Praise shall live!   170
    What Time wou'd spare, from Steel receives its date,
And Monuments, like Men, submit to Fate!
Steel cou'd the Labour of the Gods destroy,
And strike to Dust th' Imperial Tow'rs of *Troy*;
Steel cou'd the Works of mortal Pride confound,   175
And hew Triumphal Arches to the Ground.
What Wonder then, fair Nymph! thy Hairs shou'd feel
The conqu'ring Force of unresisted Steel?

---

appeared in 1709 (2 vols.). Its libels led to her arrest, but she was released
in 1710 and was soon publishing two more volumes.
167 f. Visits were an essential part of the day's routine for a fashionable
woman. They took place in the evening, and the lady was attended by
servants bearing lights. An 'essential point' of the visit was its appointed
day (*Tatler* 262) – 'solemn' is therefore a pun; it includes the sense of
solemnis, 'marked by the celebration of special observances or rites (especi-
ally of a religious character)' (OED). The visit is one of the butts of the
Tatler and *Spectator*.
171 *date*] 'end; conclusion' (Johnson).
173 f. The walls of Troy were supposed to have been built by Apollo the
Sun-god and Poseidon the Sea-god.
178 *unresisted*] irresistible. Cf. Catullus, *The Lock of Berenice*, ll. 43 ff.:

> ille quoque eversus mons est . . .
> quid facient crines, cum ferro talia cedant?

(Even that mountain was overthrown . . . What shall locks of hair do,
when such things as this yield to steel?)

CANTO IV

But anxious Cares the pensive Nymph opprest,
And secret Passions labour'd in her Breast.
Not youthful Kings in Battel seiz'd alive,
Not scornful Virgins who their Charms survive,
Not ardent Lovers robb'd of all their Bliss,   5
Not ancient Ladies when refus'd a Kiss,
Not Tyrants fierce that unrepenting die,
Not *Cynthia* when her *Manteau*'s pinn'd awry,
E'er felt such Rage, Resentment and Despair,
As Thou, sad Virgin! for thy ravish'd Hair.   10

   For, that sad moment, when the *Sylphs* withdrew,
And *Ariel* weeping from *Belinda* flew,
Umbriel, a dusky melancholy Spright,
As ever sully'd the fair face of Light,
Down to the Central Earth, his proper Scene,   15
Repair'd to search the gloomy Cave of *Spleen*.

1 Virgil, *Æneid*, 4. *At regina gravi, &c.* (P) Dryden translates:

      But anxious Cares already seiz'd the Queen.

8 The mantua, mantoe or mantua-gown was 'a loose upper Garment, now generally worn by Women, instead of a straight-body'd Gown' (E. Phillips).

13 ff. The journey to the underworld is an epic commonplace. Pope is imitating especially the description of the cave of envy in Ovid, *Metamorphoses*, ii 760 ff., which Addison translated:

      Shut from the Winds and from the wholesome Skies,
      In a deep Vale the gloomy Dungeon lies,
      Dismal and Cold, where not a Beam of Light
      Invades the Winter, or disturbs the Night. . . .

16 *Spleen*] The fashionable name for an ancient malady, the incidence of which was jealously confined to the idle rich.

Swift on his sooty Pinions flitts the *Gnome*,
And in a Vapour reach'd the dismal Dome.
No cheerful Breeze this sullen Region knows,
The dreaded *East* is all the Wind that blows.   20
Here, in a Grotto, sheltred close from Air,
And screen'd in Shades from Day's detested Glare,
She sighs for ever on her pensive Bed,
Pain at her Side, and *Megrim* at her Head.

Two Handmaids wait the Throne: Alike in Place,   25
But diff'ring far in Figure and in Face.
Here stood *Ill-nature* like an *ancient Maid*,
Her wrinkled Form in *Black* and *White* array'd;
With store of Pray'rs, for Mornings, Nights, and Noons,
Her Hand is fill'd; her Bosom with Lampoons.   30

There *Affectation* with a sickly Mien
Shows in her Cheek the Roses of Eighteen,
Practis'd to Lisp, and hang the Head aside,
Faints into Airs, and languishes with Pride;

18 *Vapour*] Pope puns on vapour(s) again at ll. 39 and 59 below. The spleen was also called the vapours and a misty climate was supposed to induce it.

Dome] in its meaning of (dignified) building (Latin *domus*).

20 The east wind was considered to provoke spleen.

21 f. Burton notes in the *Anatomy of Melancholy* that one of the symptoms of melancholy (the Elizabethan name for the spleen) is 'Solitariness, avoiding of light'.

24 The organ called the spleen is at the left side of the body; megrim, or migraine, is a 'Disorder of the head' (Johnson), a severe headache: Pope places his allegorical figures accordingly. The 1714 editions, however, read '*Languor*' for '*Megrim*'.

25 *wait*] = wait on, 'to be in readiness to receive orders' (OED).

27 ff. Ill-nature has two categories; into the *white* one she puts the purely virtuous. It is therefore unoccupied. The rest of mankind go into the *black*.

On the rich Quilt sinks with becoming Woe,   35
Wrapt in a Gown, for Sickness, and for Show.
The Fair-ones feel such Maladies as these,
When each new Night-Dress gives a new Disease.
  A constant *Vapour* o'er the Palace flies;
Strange Phantoms rising as the Mists arise;   40
Dreadful, as Hermit's Dreams in haunted Shades,
Or bright as Visions of expiring Maids.
Now glaring Fiends, and Snakes on rolling Spires,
Pale Spectres, gaping Tombs, and Purple Fires:
Now Lakes of liquid Gold, *Elysian* Scenes,   45
And Crystal Domes, and Angels in Machines.

39 *Vapour*] See note on iv 18 above.

40 ff. Hallucinations presenting such gloomy or hectic phantoms were common symptoms of the spleen.

41 f. Pope writes to Lady Mary Wortley Montagu, 5 Feb. [1716–17]: 'I am foolish again; and methinks I am imitating, in my ravings, the dreams of splenetic enthusiasts and solitaires, who fall in love with saints, and fancy themselves in the favour of angels and spirits, whom they can never see or touch.'

43 *Spires*] Spirals.

43 ff. Starting from the usual hallucinatory symptoms of the spleen, Pope leads on to a satiric catalogue of the scenic effects of contemporary opera and pantomime. (Cf. *Dunciad*, iii 231 ff.) In Mountford's *Life and Death of Doctor Faustus. Made into a Farce* (1697), 'Good and bad angels descend ... a Woman Devil rises: Fire-works about whirles round, and sinks [*sic*] ... Throne of Heaven appears ... Hell is discovered'; in D'Urfey's opera, *Wonders of the Sun* (1706), 'The Scene [is] a Luminous Country, adorn'd with Gorgeous Rays of the Sun'; in *The Necromancer; or, Harlequin Doctor Faustus* (9th edition, 1731), 'an Infernal Spirit rises. [There are] angels in Machines [i.e., mechanical scenic contrivances] [and] pale Spectres', and the spirits of Hero and Leander appear about to cross the Styx. Pope presumably also intends a particular gibe at Addison whose opera, *Rosamond*, III i, has 'a grotto, Henry asleep, a cloud descends, in it two angels'.

Unnumber'd Throngs on ev'ry side are seen
Of Bodies chang'd to various Forms by *Spleen*.
Here living *Teapots* stand, one Arm held out,
One bent; the Handle this, and that the Spout: 50
A Pipkin there like *Homer*'s *Tripod* walks;
Here sighs a Jar, and there a Goose-pye talks;
Men prove with Child, as pow'rful Fancy works,
And Maids turn'd Bottels, call aloud for Corks.

Safe past the *Gnome* thro' this fantastick Band,   55
A Branch of healing *Spleenwort* in his hand.
Then thus addrest the Pow'r – Hail wayward Queen!

47–54 These metamorphoses represent illusions commonly suffered by the splenetic.

51 *See* Homer's *Iliad*, 18, *of* Vulcan's *Walking tripods*. (P) The passage in Pope's translation (ll. 40 ff.) runs:

> Full twenty Tripods for his Hall he fram'd,
> That plac'd on living Wheels of massy Gold
> (Wond'rous to tell), instinct with Spirit roll'd,
> From Place to Place, around the blest Abodes,
> Self-mov'd, obedient to the Beck of Gods.

Pipkin] 'a small earthen boiler' (Johnson).

52 *Goose-pye*] *Alludes to a real fact, a Lady of distinction imagin'd herself in this condition.* (P)

53 'The fanciful person here alluded to, was Dr Edward Pelling [d. 1718], one of the chaplains to K. Charles II. James II. William III. and Queen Anne' (Steevens, *Supplement to Shakespeare's Plays*, 1780).

56 *Spleenwort*] This herb was considered to cure the spleen. Æneas carried the golden bough as a passport to Hades.

57 ff. This speech, which embodies common symptoms of the spleen, is built on the model of Nisus' speech to Luna (*Æneid*, ix 404 ff.) which Dryden had translated as follows:

> 'Guardian of Groves, and Goddess of the Night;
> Fair Queen,' he said, 'direct my Dart aright:
> If e're my Pious Father, for my sake

Who rule the Sex to Fifty from Fifteen,
Parent of Vapors and of Female Wit,
Who give th' *Hysteric* or *Poetic* Fit,   60
On various Tempers act by various ways,
Make some take Physick, others scribble Plays;
Who cause the Proud their Visits to delay,
And send the Godly in a Pett, to pray.
A Nymph there is, that all thy Pow'r disdains,   65
And thousands more in equal Mirth maintains.
But oh! if e'er thy *Gnome* could spoil a Grace,
Or raise a Pimple on a beauteous Face,
Like Citron-Waters Matrons' Cheeks inflame,
Or change Complexions at a losing Game;   70
If e'er with airy Horns I planted Heads,
Or rumpled Petticoats, or tumbled Beds,
Or caus'd Suspicion when no Soul was rude,
Or discompos'd the Head-dress of a Prude,
Or e'er to costive Lap-Dog gave Disease,   75
Which not the Tears of brightest Eyes could ease:
Hear me, and touch *Belinda* with Chagrin;
That single Act gives half the World the Spleen.

Did grateful Off'rings on thy Altars make;
Or I increas'd them with my Silvan toils,
And hung thy Holy Roofs with Salvage Spoils;
Give me to scatter these' . . .

59–62 Melancholy was supposed to accompany creative genius. The *Tatler* and *Spectator* always treated the spleen as a malady of both sexes. Pope restricts it entirely to women (except for l. 53). For 'Vapors' see note on iv 18 above.

63 A delayed visit is the cause of the mock trial in *Tatler* 262.

69 *Citron-Waters*] 'Aqua vitæ [brandy] distilled with the rind of citrons' (Johnson).

70 See iii 89 ff. above.

The Goddess with a discontented Air
Seems to reject him, tho' she grants his Pray'r.   80
A wondrous Bag with both her Hands she binds,
Like that where once *Ulysses* held the Winds;
There she collects the Force of Female Lungs,
Sighs, Sobs, and Passions, and the War of Tongues.
A Vial next she fills with Fainting Fears,   85
Soft Sorrows, melting Griefs, and flowing Tears.
The *Gnome* rejoicing bears her Gifts away.
Spreads his black Wings, and slowly mounts to Day.
    Sunk in *Thalestris*' Arms the Nymph he found,
Her Eyes dejected and her Hair unbound.   90
Full o'er their Heads the swelling Bag he rent,
And all the Furies issued at the Vent.
Belinda burns with more than mortal Ire,
And fierce *Thalestris* fans the rising Fire.
O wretched Maid! she spreads her Hands, and cry'd,   95

80 'Finely intimating that way-ward humour, which inclines people under
the influence of this *queen* to mortify by refusal, even when the request is
in unison with their own disposition' (Wakefield).
82 Cf. *Odyssey*, x 19 ff.
89 Thalestris was the Queen of the Amazons, 'of an admirable Beauty,
and strong Body, greatly honour'd in her own Country for [her] Brave
and Manly Spirit'.
    Here she represents Lady Browne, the wife of Sir George (Sir Plume).
90 Unbound hair is a sign of distress in the epics.
95 ff. Cf. Nestor's speech to the Greeks, *Iliad*, vii 145 ff.

> ... What Grief, what shame
> Attend on Greece, and all the Grecian name?
> How shall alas her hoary heroes mourn
> Their sons degenerate, and their race a scorn?
> What tears shall down thy silver beard be roll'd,
> Of Peleus, old in arms, in wisdom old! ...
> Gods! should he see our warriors trembling stand,

(While *Hampton*'s Ecchos, wretched Maid! reply'd)
Was it for this you took such constant Care
The *Bodkin*, *Comb*, and *Essence* to prepare;
For this your Locks in Paper-Durance bound,
For this with tort'ring Irons wreath'd around?   100
For this with Fillets strain'd your tender Head,
And bravely bore the double Loads of Lead?
Gods! shall the Ravisher display your Hair,
While the Fops envy, and the Ladies stare!
Honour forbid! at whose unrival'd Shrine   105
Ease, Pleasure, Virtue, All, our Sex resign.
Methinks already I your Tears survey,
Already hear the horrid things they say,
Already see you a degraded Toast,
And all your Honour in a Whisper lost!   110

> And trembling all before one trembling hand;
> How would he lift his aged arms on high,
> Lament inglorious Greece, and beg to die!
> Oh! would to all th' immortal pow'rs above,
> Minerva, Phœbus, and almighty Jove!
> Years might again roll back, my youth renew,
> And give this arm the spring which once it knew. . . .

98 Cf. note on ii 128 above.

99 ff. The imagery is from incarceration and torture. 'The curl papers of ladies' hair used to be fastened with strips of pliant lead' (Croker).

107 Cf. *Iliad*, xxii 53 f. (Hecuba is foreseeing the death of Hector):

> Methinks already I behold thee slain,
> And stretch'd beneath that Fury of the Plain.

108 Cf. Garth's *Dispensary*: And never mean the peevish Things we say.

109 A 'toast' is 'A celebrated woman whose health is often drunk' (Johnson).

110 Cf. Pope's letter to Caryll, 21 Dec. 1712: 'More men's reputations I believe are whispered away, than any otherways destroyed.'

How shall I, then, your helpless Fame defend?
'Twill then be Infamy to seem your Friend!
And shall this Prize, th' inestimable Prize,
Exposed thro' Crystal to the gazing Eyes,
And heighten'd by the Diamond's circling Rays,   115
On that Rapacious Hand for ever blaze?
Sooner shall Grass in *Hide*-Park *Circus* grow,
And Wits take Lodgings in the Sound of *Bow*;
Sooner let Earth, Air, Sea, to *Chaos* fall,
Men, Monkies, Lap-dogs, Parrots, perish all!   120

114 f. The Baron is foreseen as having had some of Belinda's lock set in a ring.

117 ff. Cf. Virgil, *Eclogues*, i 60 ff., which Dryden translates thus:

> Th' Inhabitants of Seas and Skies shall change,
> And Fish on Shoar and Stags in Air shall range,
> The banish'd *Parthian* dwell on *Arar's* brink,
> And the blue *German* shall the *Tigris* drink:
> E're I, forsaking Gratitude and Truth,
> Forget the Figure of that Godlike Youth.

Garth (*Dispensary*) had already parodied this passage:

> The tow'ring *Alps* shall sooner sink to Vales,
> And *Leaches*, in our Glasses, swell to *Whales*;
> Or *Norwich* trade in Implements of Steel,
> And *Bromingham* in Stuffs and Druggets deal.

117 See note on i 44 above. Lady Malapert in Southerne's *Maids last Prayer* (iv i) longs for something 'More wholesome, and diverting, than . . . the dusty Mill-Horse driving in *Hide-Park*'. The amount of dust in the Ring is frequently complained of, or noticed satirically for its contrast to fresh air, though there were organized attempts to keep it down by water-carts. One writer on London parks produces an unwitting annotation of this line: 'It is probable then [during the Plague] that the grass grew in the Ring, as well as in the streets of the City.'

118 The City with its solid brick citizens' houses had become almost wholly mercantile. The fashionable quarter had already shifted west.

She said; then raging to *Sir Plume* repairs,
And bids her *Beau* demand the precious Hairs:
(*Sir Plume*, of *Amber Snuff-box* justly vain,
And the nice Conduct of a *clouded Cane*)
With earnest Eyes, and round unthinking Face,   125
He first the Snuff-box open'd, then the Case,
And thus broke out – 'My Lord, why, what the Devil?
'Z——ds! damn the Lock! 'fore Gad, you must be civil!
'Plague on't! 'tis past a Jest – nay prithee, Pox!
'Give her the Hair' – he spoke, and rapp'd his Box.   130
    It grieves me much (reply'd the Peer again)
Who speaks so well shou'd ever speak in vain.
But by this Lock, this sacred Lock I swear,
(Which never more shall join its parted Hair,
Which never more its Honours shall renew,   135

121 *Sir Plume*] Sir George Browne (see Introduction, p. 6 above). He was the cousin of Arabella's mother.

123, 126 See note on iii 17 above.

124 *nice Conduct*] exquisite management. *Tatler* 103 had ridiculed the mannerisms of beaux with their canes, some of which are 'curiously clouded' and amber-headed. The snuff-box is included in the satire. Johnson defines his fourth meaning of *cloud* as to 'variegate with dark veins'.

127 ff. Sir Plume speaks the language of the 'common Swearer' in *Tatler* 13.

128 *Z——ds*] corrupted from *God's wounds*.

133 ff. *In allusion to* Achilles's *Oath in* Homer, *Iliad, i* [309 ff.]. (P)

> Now by this sacred Sceptre, hear me swear,
> Which never more shall Leaves or Blossoms bear,
> Which sever'd from the Trunk (as I from thee)
> On the bare Mountains left its Parent Tree . . .

135, 140 *Honours*] Cowley had defined them as '*Beauties*, which make things *Honoured*; in which sense *Virgil* often uses the word, and delights in it:

> *Et lætos oculis afflârat Honores'*

Clipt from the lovely Head where late it grew)
That while my Nostrils draw the vital Air,
This Hand, which won it, shall for ever wear.
He spoke, and speaking, in proud Triumph spread
The long-contended Honours of her Head.   140
    But *Umbriel*, hateful *Gnome*! forbears not so;
He breaks the Vial whence the Sorrows flow.
Then see! the *Nymph* in beauteous Grief appears,
Her Eyes half-languishing, half-drown'd in Tears;
On her heav'd Bosom hung her drooping Head,   145
Which, with a Sigh, she rais'd; and thus she said.
    For ever curs'd be this detested Day.
Which snatch'd my best, my fav'rite Curl away!
Happy! ah ten times happy, had I been,
If *Hampton-Court* these Eyes had never seen!   150
Yet am not I the first mistaken Maid,
By Love of *Courts* to num'rous Ills betray'd.
Oh had I rather un-admir'd remain'd
In some lone Isle, or distant *Northern* Land;
Where the gilt *Chariot* never marks the Way,   155

137 Cf. *Æneid*, iv 336: 'dum spiritus hos regit artus' (while breath still
sways these limbs).

141 f. *These two lines are additional; and assign the cause of the different
operation of the Passions of the two Ladies. The poem went on before without
that distinction, as without any Machinery to the end of the Canto.* (P) 'At verse
91, Umbriel empties the bag which contains the angry passions over the
heads of Thalestris and Belinda. At verse 142 he breaks the phial of sorrow
over Belinda alone, whence Belinda's anger is turned to grief, and Thalestris
remains indignant' (EC).

147 ff. This speech is modelled on Achilles' lament for Patroclus, *Iliad*,
xviii 107 ff.

149 f. An adaptation of Dido's cry, *Æneid*, iv 657 f.

155 Contemporary engravings of chariots always show them leaving deep
ruts in the earth of the roads.

Where none learn *Ombre*, none e'er taste *Bohea*!
There kept my Charms conceal'd from mortal Eye,
Like Roses that in Desarts bloom and die.
What mov'd my Mind with youthful Lords to rome?
O had I stay'd, and said my Pray'rs at home!   160
'Twas this, the Morning *Omens* seem'd to tell;
Thrice from my trembling hand the *Patch-box* fell;
The tott'ring *China* shook without a Wind,
Nay, *Poll* sate mute, and *Shock* was most Unkind!
A *Sylph* too warn'd me of the Threats of Fate,   165
In mystic Visions, now believ'd too late!
See the poor Remnants of these slighted Hairs!
My hands shall rend what ev'n thy Rapine spares:
These, in two sable Ringlets taught to break,
Once gave new Beauties to the snowie Neck.   170
The Sister-Lock now sits uncouth, alone,
And in its Fellow's Fate foresees its own;
Uncurl'd it hangs, the fatal Sheers demands;
And tempts once more thy sacrilegious Hands.
Oh hadst thou, Cruel! been content to seize   175
Hairs less in sight, or any Hairs but these!

156 *Bohea*] 'A species of tea, of higher colour, and more astringent tastes
than green tea' (Johnson).
166 'Nothing is more common in the poets, than to introduce omens as
preceding some important and dreadful event' (Warton); Virgil has
strongly described those that preceded the death of Dido.
169 *sable*] According to the three extant portraits, Arabella Fermor's hair
was fair auburn. 'Fair Tresses' are mentioned at ii 27 above, though Pope
may not there be referring to colour and certainly is not referring in
particular to Arabella's hair. Black hair was most in fashion, and black lead
combs were used to darken hair considered too fair.

CANTO V

She said: the pitying Audience melt in Tears,
But *Fate* and *Jove* had stopp'd the *Baron*'s Ears.
In vain *Thalestris* with Reproach assails,
For who can move when fair *Belinda* fails?
Not half so fixt the *Trojan* cou'd remain,   5
While *Anna* begg'd and *Dido* rag'd in vain.
Then grave *Clarissa* graceful wav'd her Fan;

1 ff. Pope is imitating *Æneid*, iv to which he refers at 5 f. At 2 he adapts
440 of Virgil:

> Fata obstant, placidasque viri deus obstruit aures,

which Dryden had translated thus:

> Fate, and the God, had stop'd his Ears to Love.

7 *Clarissa*] *A new Character introduced in the subsequent Editions, to open
more clearly the* MORAL *of the Poem, in a parody of the speech of Sarpedon to
Glaucus in Homer.* (P) Clarissa is a new character in the sense that she has
a spoken part, but she appeared in the 1712 version at i 107 where, as in
the 1714 version, iii 127, she lent the Baron her scissors.

Pope's translation of the speech runs as follows in the version included
in the *Iliad* (xii 371 ff.):

> Why boast we, *Glaucus*! our extended Reign,
> Where *Xanthus*' Streams enrich the *Lycian* Plain,
> Our num'rous Herds that range the fruitful Field,
> And Hills where Vines their purple Harvest yield,
> Our foaming Bowls with purer Nectar crown'd,
> Our Feasts enhanc'd with Music's sprightly Sound?
> Why on those Shores are we met with Joy survey'd,
> Admir'd as Heroes, and as Gods obey'd?
> Unless great Acts superior Merit prove,
> And vindicate the bount'ous Pow'rs above.
> 'Tis ours, the Dignity they give, to grace;
> The first in Valour, as the first in Place.
> That when with wond'ring Eyes our martial Bands

Silence ensu'd, and thus the Nymph began.
Say, why are Beauties prais'd and honour'd most,
The wise Man's Passion, and the vain Man's Toast?   10
Why deck'd with all that Land and Sea afford,
Why Angels call'd, and Angel-like ador'd?
Why round our Coaches crowd the white-glov'd Beaus,
Why bows the Side-box from its inmost Rows?
How vain are all these Glories, all our Pains,   15
Unless good Sense preserve what Beauty gains:
That Men may say, when we the Front-box grace,
Behold the first in Virtue, as in Face!
Oh! if to dance all Night, and dress all Day,
Charm'd the Small-pox, or chas'd old Age away;   20

Behold our Deeds transcending our Commands,
Such, they may cry, deserve the sov'reign State,
Whom those that envy, dare not imitate!
Could all our Care elude the gloomy Grave,
Which claims no less the fearful than the brave,
For Lust of Fame I should not vainly dare
In fighting Fields, nor urge thy Soul to War.
But since, alas! ignoble Age must come,
Disease, and Death's inexorable Doom;
The Life which others pay, let us bestow,
And give to Fame what we to Nature owe;
Brave tho' we fall, and honour'd if we live,
Or let us Glory gain, or Glory give!

13 f., 17 'Representatives of a *British* Audience' are described by Steele as
'Three of the Fair Sex [for] the Front-Boxes . . . Two Gentlemen of
Wit and Pleasure for the Side-Boxes . . . Three Substantial Citizens for the
Pit'; cf. v 17 below.

16, 30 f. *good Sense . . . good Humour*] Philosophic praise of these qualities
is found at least as early as Montaigne, and they are constantly counselled
by Shaftesbury, the *Tatler*, and the *Spectator*.

20 *Small-pox*] The terrors of this disease may be gauged from the records

Who would not scorn what Huswife's Cares produce,
Or who would learn one earthly Thing of Use?
To patch, nay ogle, might become a Saint,
Nor could it sure be such a Sin to paint.
But since, alas! frail Beauty must decay,   25
Curl'd or uncurl'd, since Locks will turn to grey,
Since painted, or not painted, all shall fade,
And she who scorns a Man, must die a Maid;
What then remains, but well our Pow'r to use,
And keep good Humour still whate'er we lose?   30
And trust me, Dear! good Humour can prevail,
When Airs, and Flights, and Screams, and Scolding fail.
Beauties in vain their pretty Eyes may roll;
Charms strike the Sight, but Merit wins the Soul.

   So spoke the Dame, but no Applause ensu'd;   35
Belinda frown'd, Thalestris call'd her Prude.
To Arms, to Arms! the fierce Virago cries,
And swift as Lightning to the Combat flies.
All side in Parties, and begin th' Attack;
Fans clap, Silks russle, and tough Whalebones crack;   40

---

of the Petre family: when the Hon. John Petre died in 1762 (æt. 24) the
Gent. Mag. noted him as 'the 18th person of that family that has died of the
small pox in 27 years'. The Lord Petre of the poem had died of it in 1713,
so that this line would have especial point.

35 *It is a verse frequently repeated in* Homer *after any speech,*

         So spoke – and all the Heroes applauded. (P)

37 *From hence the first Edition goes on to the Conclusion, except a very few short
insertions added, to keep the Machinery in view to the end of the poem.* (P)

37 f. *Virago*] 'A female warriour, a woman with the qualities of a man'
(Johnson). Camilla in Dryden's *Æneid* (vii 1098 and xi 768) is called 'the
fierce *Virago*'.

40 'Women are armed with Fans as Men with Swords, and sometimes do

Heroes' and Heroins' Shouts confus'dly rise,
And base, and treble Voices strike the Skies.
No common Weapons in their Hands are found,
Like Gods they fight, nor dread a mortal Wound.
  So when bold *Homer* makes the Gods engage,   45
And heav'nly Breasts with human Passions rage;
'Gainst *Pallas*, *Mars*; *Latona*, *Hermes* Arms;
And all *Olympus* rings with loud Alarms.
Jove's Thunder roars, Heav'n trembles all around;
Blue *Neptune* storms, the bellowing Deeps resound;   50
Earth shakes her nodding Tow'rs, the Ground gives way;
And the pale Ghosts start at the Flash of Day!

---

more Execution with them' (*Spectator*, 102, which describes the practice
of 'discharging' fans loud enough to make the 'crack' resemble the 'Report
of a Pocket-Pistol'). The whale-bones are those of the petticoats: cf ii 120
above.

45 Homer, *Iliad* 20 [91 ff.]. (P) Pope's translation runs):

> First silver-shafted *Phœbus* took the Plain
> Against blue *Neptune*, Monarch of the Main:
> The God of Arms his Giant Bulk display'd,
> Oppos'd to *Pallas*, War's triumphant Maid.
> Against *Latona* march'd the Son of *May*;
> The quiver'd *Dian*, Sister of the Day,
> (Her golden Arrows sounding at her side)
> *Saturnia*, Majesty of Heav'n, defy'd.
> With fiery *Vulcan* last in Battle stands
> The sacred Flood that rolls on golden Sands.

47 The juxtaposition of proper nouns to suggest stridency and collision is
the method of Ovid and Statius (and not of Homer). Cf. the battle in
Thebaid, vii where 640 ff. read:

> . . . sternunt alterna furentes
> Hippomedon Sybarin, Pylium Periphanta Menoeceus,
> Parthenopaeus Ityn . . .

Triumphant *Umbriel* on a Sconce's Height
Clapt his glad Wings, and sate to view the Fight:
Propt on their Bodkin Spears, the Sprights survey   55
The growing Combat, or assist the Fray.
    While thro' the Press enrag'd *Thalestris* flies,
And scatters Death around from both her Eyes,
A *Beau* and *Witling* perish'd in the Throng,
One dy'd in *Metaphor*, and one in *Song*.   60
O cruel Nymph! a living Death I bear,
Cry'd *Dapperwit*, and sunk beside his Chair.
A mournful Glance Sir *Fopling* upwards cast,
Those Eyes are made so killing – was his last:

53–6 *These four lines added, for the reason before mentioned.* (P)

53 f. Minerva *in like manner, during the Battle of* Ulysses *with the Suitors in* Odyss. [xxii 261 f.] *perches on a beam of the roof to behold it.* (P)

Sconce] 'A pensile candlestick' (Johnson).

55 'Like the heroes in Homer, when they are Spectators of a combat' (Warton, ed.): see *Iliad*, xiv 533.

Bodkin] Cf. note on ii 128 above.

60 Cf. John Sheffield, Duke of Buckingham's *Essay on Poetry*, concerning the speech of heroic drama:

> Or else like Bells, eternally they chime,
> They *sigh* in *simile* and *die* in *Rhime*.

62 Dapperwit is living up to his character in Wycherley's *Love in a Wood*; see, e.g., II i.

63 *Sir Fopling*] The chief character in Etherege's *Man of Mode, or Sir Fopling Flutter*, one of 'our most applauded plays' (*Spectator*, 65).

64 *The Words in a Song in the Opera of* Camilla. (P) This, the most famous opera of Marc' Antonio Buononcini, brother of Handel's rival, was first performed in England on 30 April 1706, and performed fifty-four times during 1706–9. The song referred to is sung by Tullia in Act III and opens:

> These Eyes are made so killing
> That all who look must dye.

Thus on *Meander*'s flow'ry Margin lies   65
Th' expiring Swan, and as he sings he dies.
    When bold Sir *Plume* had drawn *Clarissa* down,
Chloe stept in, and kill'd him with a Frown;
She smil'd to see the doughty Hero slain,
But at her Smile, the Beau reviv'd again.   70
    Now *Jove* suspends his golden Scales in Air,
Weighs the Men's Wits against the Lady's Hair;
The doubtful Beam long nods from side to side;
At length the Wits mount up, the Hairs subside.
    See fierce *Belinda* on the *Baron* flies,   75
With more than usual Lightning in her Eyes;
Nor fear'd the Chief th'unequal Fight to try,
Who sought no more than on his Foe to die.
But this bold Lord, with manly Strength indu'd,
She with one Finger and a Thumb subdu'd: 80

65 f. Ov. Ep. [vii 1 f.].

> *Sic ubi fata vocant, udis abjectus in herbis,*
> *Ad vada Mæandri concinit albus olor.*

(P) (Thus, at the summons of fate, casting himself down amid the watery
grasses by the shallows of Mæander, sings the white swan.)

71 ff. *Vid.* Homer, *Iliad* 8 and Virgil, *Æneid* 12. (P) Dryden, *Æneid*, xii
1054 ff. reads:

> Jove sets the Beam; in either Scale he lays
> The Champions Fate, and each exactly weighs.
> On this side Life, and lucky Chance ascends:
> Loaded with Death, that other Scale descends.

The device is common in epics. Pope mocks the epic and, at the same
time, man: Jove's scales show the wits of beaux outweighed by a lock of
hair.

76 Cf. i 144 above.

78 The original wit of this threadbare innuendo is renewed when the
context is a battle.

Just where the Breath of Life his Nostrils drew,
A Charge of *Snuff* the wily Virgin threw;
The *Gnomes* direct, to ev'ry Atome just,
The pungent Grains of titillating Dust.
Sudden, with starting Tears each Eye o'erflows, 85
And the high Dome re-ecchoes to his Nose.

  Now meet thy Fate, incens'd *Belinda* cry'd,
And drew a deadly *Bodkin* from her Side.
(The same, his ancient Personage to deck,
Her great great Grandsire wore about his Neck 90
In three *Seal-Rings*; which after, melted down,
Form'd a vast *Buckle* for his Widow's Gown:
Her infant Grandame's *Whistle* next it grew,
The *Bells* she gingled, and the *Whistle* blew;
Then in a *Bodkin* grac'd her Mother's Hairs, 95
Which long she wore, and now *Belinda* wears.)

  Boast not my Fall (he cry'd) insulting Foe!
Thou by some other shalt be laid as low.
Nor think, to die dejects my lofty Mind;
All that I dread, is leaving you behind! 100
Rather than so, ah let me still survive,

---

83 f. *These two lines added for the above reason.* (P)
88 *Bodkin*] See note on ii 128 above.
89 f. *In Imitation of the Progress of* Agamemnon's *Scepter in* Homer, *Il.* 2.
(P) Pope translates:

> The Golden Sceptre, of Celestial Frame,
> By *Vulcan* form'd, from *Jove* to *Hermes* came:
> To *Pelops* He th'immortal Gift resign'd;
> Th'immortal Gift great *Pelops* left behind,
> In *Atreus*' Hand; which not with *Atreus* ends,
> To rich *Thyestes* next the Prize descends;
> And now the Mark of *Agamemnon's* Reign,
> Subjects all *Argos*, and controuls the Main.

And burn in *Cupid*'s Flames, – but burn alive.

  Restore the Lock! she cries, and all around

Restore the Lock! the vaulted Roofs rebound.

Not fierce *Othello* in so loud a Strain   105

Roar'd for the Handkerchief that caus'd his Pain.

But see how oft Ambitious Aims are cross'd,

And Chiefs contend 'till all the Prize is lost!

The Lock, obtain'd with Guilt, and kept with Pain,

In ev'ry place is sought, but sought in vain: 110

With such a Prize no Mortal must be blest,

So Heav'n decrees! with Heav'n who can contest?

  Some thought it mounted to the Lunar Sphere,

Since all things lost on Earth, are treasur'd there.

105 Rymer's criticism of *Othello* appeared in *A Short View of Tragedy* (1693). His running commentary on the play over-emphasizes the part of the handkerchief: 'So much ado, so much stress, so much passion and repetition about an Handkerchief!'

114 ff. *Vid.* Ariosto, Canto 34. (P) Astolfo journeys to the moon in search of Orlando's lost wits, and finds

> A mighty masse of things strangely confus'd,
> Things that on earth were lost, or were abus'd.

Among these are

> The vowes that sinners make, and never pay,

gifts given to princes, 'fond loves',

> Large promises that Lords make, and forget . . .
> The fruitlesse almes that men give when they die.

Here 'mans wit' is kept in jars. Astolfo finds Orlando's wit and that of other great men:

> Some lose their wit with love, some with ambition,
> Some running to the sea, great wealth to get,
> Some following Lords, and men of high condition,
> And some in faire jewels rich and costly set:
> One hath desire to prove a rare Magician,

There Heroes' Wits are kept in pondrous Vases,   115
And Beaus' in *Snuff-boxes* and *Tweezer-Cases*.
There broken Vows, and Death-bed Alms are found,
And Lovers' Hearts with ends of Riband bound;
The Courtier's Promises, and Sick Man's Pray'rs,
The Smiles of Harlots, and the Tears of Heirs,   120
Cages for Gnats, and Chains to Yoak a Flea;
Dry'd Butterflies, and Tomes of Casuistry.
    But trust the Muse – she saw it upward rise,
Tho' mark'd by none but quick Poetic Eyes:
(So *Rome*'s great Founder to the Heav'ns withdrew,   125
To *Proculus* alone confess'd in view.)

            And some with Poetrie their wit forget,
            Another thinks to be an Alcumist,
            Till all be spent; and he his number mist.

(All the above quotations are from Harington's translation ed. 1634.) Pope modernizes Ariosto's instances and makes them more particularly concrete.
115 *Vases*] The pronunciation of Pope's day is still current in America.
116 *Tweezer-Cases*] Cf. *Tatler*, 142: 'his Tweezer-Cases are incomparable: You shall have one not much bigger than your Finger, with seventeen several Instruments in it, all necessary every Hour of the Day, during the whole Course of a Man's Life'.
122 *Dry'd Butterflies*] The 'virtuosos' of the time and their natural history collections are often satirized.
    Casuistry] The minute philosophy of the Middle Ages and the earlier seventeenth century has fallen into disrepute.
125 f. 'Romulus was said to have disappeared during an eclipse of the sun while he was addressing the senate. To disarm suspicion, the senators caused it to be reported that he had been caught up to heaven; the report was credited the more readily when Julius Proculus declared that Romulus had appeared to him on the road near Alba, and had confirmed this, and ordered him to tell the Romans to sacrifice to him under the name of Quirinus' (Holden).

A sudden Star, it shot thro' liquid Air,
And drew behind a radiant *Trail of Hair*.
Not *Berenice*'s Locks first rose so bright,
The Heav'ns bespangling with dishevel'd Light.   130
The *Sylphs* behold it kindling as it flies,
And pleas'd pursue its Progress thro' the Skies.

This the *Beau-monde* shall from the *Mall* survey,
And hail with Musick its propitious Ray.
This, the blest Lover shall for *Venus* take,   135
And send up Vows from *Rosamonda*'s Lake.

127 *liquid*] in the Latin sense of clear.
127 f. Cf. Ovid, *Metamorphoses*, xv 849 f.:

> Flammiferumque trahens spatioso limite crinen
> Stella micat.

129 f. Berenice vowed to hang up her hair in the temple of Venus if her brother-husband, Ptolemy III, returned victorious from the wars. The vow was kept, and when the offering was stolen, an astrologer explained that Jupiter had made a constellation of it. Callimachus' poem on her constellated hair exists (apart from a fragment) only in the translation of Catullus.

dishevel'd] 'applicable alike to the *lock* in question, and to the radiance of the comet's *hair*' (Wakefield).

131 f. *These two lines added for the same reason to keep in view the Machinery of the Poem.* (P)

133 f. Charles II improved St James's Park by the addition of lines of trees, a canal, and the Mall. From the time when he made the Park public, the Mall rivalled the Ring as a fashionable resort. It was an enclosed walk running parallel to the front of St James's Palace, and partly devoted at first to the game of pall-mall (a kind of croquet). Sir Simon Addlepate in Wycherley's *Love in a Wood* (II i) sends for fiddlers 'to serenade the whole Park to-night'. They come and play, and there is dancing; such impromptu music and dancing were not uncommon.

136 Rosamonda's Lake, an oblong pond near the south-west corner of St James's Park, had long been 'consecrated to disastrous love, and *elegiac* poetry'.

This *Partridge* soon shall view in cloudless Skies,
When next he looks thro' *Galilæo*'s Eyes;
And hence th' Egregious Wizard shall foredoom
The Fate of *Louis*, and the Fall of *Rome*.   140
  Then cease, bright Nymph! to mourn thy ravish'd
    Hair
Which adds new Glory to the shining Sphere!
Not all the Tresses that fair Head can boast
Shall draw such Envy as the Lock you lost.
For, after all the Murders of your Eye,   145
When, after Millions slain, your self shall die;
When those fair Suns shall sett, as sett they must,
And all those Tresses shall be laid in Dust;
This Lock, the Muse shall consecrate to Fame,
And mid'st the Stars inscribe *Belinda*'s Name!   150

FINIS

137 John Partridge *was a ridiculous Star-gazer, who in his Almanacks every year, never fail'd to predict the downfall of the Pope, and the King of France then at war with the English.* (P) Partridge (1644–1715) is immortalized by Swift's practical joke: see *Predictions for the Year 1708* by *Isaac Bickerstaff*, etc.
138 Galileo improved the newly invented telescope and by its aid inaugurated a new era in the history of astronomy.
142 *Sphere*] 'This was among the words pronounced in Pope's day in continental fashion "sphare". It is found at the end of a line eight times in Pope and only once (*Essay on Man*, i 202) is it rimed otherwise' (Holden).
147 f. 'The poem concludes, as it had opened (Canto i 13), with a comparison of the brightness of Belinda's eyes to that of the sun' (Holden). At ii 3, she was 'the Rival of his Beams'. Sidney in the *Arcades* calls eyes 'those suns'.
148 ff. Cf. Spenser, *Amoretti*, lxxv 9 ff.:

      Not so, (quod I) let baser things devize
        to dy in dust, but you shall live by fame:
        my verse your vertues rare shall eternize,
        and in the hevens wryte your glorious name.

APPENDIX A
The 1712 Version of the poem
THE RAPE OF THE LOCKE
AN HEROI-COMICAL POEM

Nolueram, Belinda, *tuos violare capillos,*
    Sed juvat hoc precibus me tribuisse tuis.
                    MART. Lib. 12. Ep. 86.

CANTO I

What dire Offence from Am'rous Causes springs,
What mighty Quarrels rise from Trivial Things,
I sing – This Verse to *C——l*, Muse! is due;
This, ev'n *Belinda* may vouchsafe to view:
Slight is the Subject, but not so the Praise,   5
If she inspire, and He approve my Lays.

   Say what strange Motive, Goddess! cou'd compel
A well-bred *Lord* t'assault a gentle *Belle*?
Oh say what stranger Cause, yet unexplor'd,
Cou'd make a gentle *Belle* reject a *Lord*?   10
And dwells such Rage in *softest Bosoms* then?
And lodge such daring Souls in *Little Men*?

   Sol thro' white Curtains did his Beams display,
And op'd those Eyes which brighter shine than they;
Shock just had giv'n himself the rowzing Shake   15
And Nymphs prepar'd their *Chocolate* to take;

11 In his satiric attack on bad poets, the *Peri Bathous*, Pope notes that 'the
whole Spirit of the *Bathos* shall be owing to *one choice Word that ends the
Line*'. A contemporary poet cleverly cited the present line as a good
instance of the truth of Pope's observation. Pope revises the line in the
edition of 1736, see *Rape of the Lock*, i 11 f., p. 19 above.
12 Cf. Virgil, *Georgics*, iv 83 (of the bees):

> Ingentes animos angusto in pectore versant;

Addison's translation:

> Their little bodies lodge a mighty soul;

and *Iliad*, v 999:

> Whose little Body lodg'd a mighty Mind.

Thrice the wrought Slipper knock'd against the Ground,
And striking Watches the tenth Hour resound.
Belinda rose, and 'midst attending Dames
Launch'd on the Bosom of the silver *Thames*:   20
A Train of well-drest Youths around her shone,
And ev'ry Eye was fixed on her alone;
On her white Breast a sparkling *Cross* she wore,
Which *Jews* might kiss, and Infidels adore.
Her lively Looks a sprightly Mind disclose,   25
Quick as her Eyes, and as unfixt as those:
Favours to none, to all she Smiles extends;
Oft she rejects, but never once offends.
Bright as the Sun her Eyes the Gazers strike,
And, like the Sun, they shine on all alike.   30
Yet graceful Ease, and Sweetness void of Pride,
Might hide her Faults, if *Belles* had Faults to hide:
If to her share some Female Errors fall,
Look on her Face, and you'll forgive 'em all.

    This Nymph, to the Destruction of Mankind,   35
Nourish'd two Locks, which graceful hung behind
In equal Curls, and well conspir'd to deck
With shining Ringlets her smooth Iv'ry Neck.
Love in these Labyrinths his Slaves detains,
And mighty Hearts are held in slender Chains.   40
With hairy Sprindges we the Birds betray,
Slight Lines of Hair surprize the Finny Prey,
Fair Tresses Man's Imperial Race insnare,
And Beauty draws us with a *single Hair*.

    Th'Adventrous *Baron* the bright Locks admir'd,   45
He saw, he wish'd, and to the Prize aspir'd:
Resolv'd to win, he meditates the way,
By Force to ravish, or by Fraud betray;

For when Success a Lover's Toil attends,
Few ask, if Fraud or Force attain'd his Ends. 50
　For this, ere *Phœbus* rose, he had implor'd
Propitious Heav'n, and ev'ry Pow'r ador'd,
But chiefly *Love* – to *Love* an Altar built,
Of twelve vast *French* Romances, neatly gilt.
There lay the Sword-knot *Sylvia's* Hands had sown 55
With *Flavia's* Busk that oft had rapp'd his own:
A Fan, a Garter, half a Pair of Gloves;
And all the Trophies of his former Loves.
With tender *Billet-doux* he lights the Pyre,
And breathes three am'rous Sighs to raise the Fire. 60
Then prostrate falls, and begs with ardent Eyes
Soon to obtain, and long possess the Prize:
The Pow'rs gave Ear, and granted half his Pray'r,
The rest, the Winds dispers'd in empty Air.

　Close by those Meads for ever crown'd with Flow'rs, 65
Where *Thames* with Pride surveys his rising Tow'rs,
There stands a Structure of Majestick Frame,
Which from the neighb'ring *Hampton* takes its Name.
Here *Britain's* Statesmen oft the Fall foredoom
Of Foreign Tyrants, and of Nymphs at home; 70
Here Thou, great *Anna*! whom three Realms obey,
Dost sometimes Counsel take – and sometimes *Tea*.
Hither our Nymphs and Heroes did resort,
To taste awhile the Pleasures of a Court;
In various Talk the chearful hours they past, 75
Of, who was *Bitt*, or who *Capotted* last:

56 A busk is 'A strip of wood, whalebone, steel, or other rigid material passed down the front of a corset, and used to stiffen or support it '(OED)
76 *Bitt*] = cheated at cards.
　Capotted] = scored all the tricks at cards: see OED.

This speaks the Glory of the *British Queen*,
And that describes a charming *Indian Screen*;
A third interprets Motions, Looks, and Eyes;
At ev'ry Word a Reputation dies.   80
Snuff, or the *Fan*, supply each Pause of Chatt,
With singing, laughing, ogling, and all that.
    Now, when declining from the Noon of Day,
The Sun obliquely shoots his burning Ray;
When hungry Judges soon the Sentence sign,   85
And Wretches hang that Jury-men may Dine;
When Merchants from th'*Exchange* return in Peace,
And the long Labours of the *Toilette* cease –
The Board's with Cups and Spoons, alternate, crown'd;
The Berries crackle, and the Mill turns round;   90
On shining Altars of *Japan* they raise
The silver *Lamp*, and fiery Spirits blaze;
From silver Spouts the grateful Liquors glide,
And *China*'s Earth receives the smoking Tyde:
At once they gratifie their Smell and Taste,   95
While frequent Cups prolong the rich Repast.
Coffee, (which makes the Politician wise,
And see thro' all things with his half shut Eyes)
Sent up in Vapours to the *Baron*'s Brain
New Stratagems, the radiant Locke to gain.   100
Ah cease rash Youth! desist ere 'tis too late,
Fear the just Gods, and think of *Scylla*'s Fate!
Chang'd to a Bird, and sent to flitt in Air,
She dearly pays for *Nisus*' injur'd Hair!
    But when to Mischief Mortals bend their Mind,   105
How soon fit Instruments of Ill they find!
Just then, *Clarissa* drew with tempting Grace

103 *Vide* Ovid, *Metamorphoses*, 8. (P)

A two-edg'd Weapon from her shining Case;
So Ladies in Romance assist their Knight,
Present the Spear, and arm him for the Fight. 110
He takes the Gift with rev'rence, and extends
The little Engine on his Fingers' Ends,
This just behind *Belinda*'s Neck he spread,
As o'er the fragrant Steams she bends her Head:
He first expands the glitt'ring *Forfex* wide 115
T'inclose the Lock; then joins it, to divide;
One fatal stroke the sacred Hair does sever
From the fair Head, for ever, and for ever!

The living Fires come flashing from her Eyes,
And Screams of Horror rend th'affrighted Skies. 120
Not louder Shrieks by Dames to Heav'n are cast,
When Husbands die, or *Lap-dogs* breathe their last,
Or when rich *China* Vessels fal'n from high,
In glittring Dust and painted Fragments lie!

Let Wreaths of triumph now my Temples twine, 125
(The Victor cry'd) the glorious Prize is mine!
While Fish in Streams, or Birds delight in Air,
Or in a Coach and Six the *British* Fair,
As long as *Atalantis* shall be read,
Or the small Pillow grace a Lady's Bed, 130
While *Visits* shall be paid on solemn Days,
When num'rous Wax-lights in bright Order blaze,
While Nymphs take Treats, or Assignations give,
So long my Honour, Name and Praise shall live!

What Time wou'd spare, from Steel receives its date, 135
And Monuments, like Men, submit to Fate!
Steel did the Labour of the Gods destroy,
And strike to Dust th'aspiring Tow'rs of *Troy*;
Steel cou'd the Works of mortal Pride confound,

And hew Triumphal Arches to the ground.　　140
What Wonder then, fair Nymph! thy Hairs shou'd feel
The conqu'ring Force of unresisted Steel?

CANTO II

But anxious Cares the pensive Nymph opprest,
And secret Passions labour'd in her Breast.
Not youthful Kings in Battel seiz'd alive,
Not scornful Virgins who their Charms survive,
Not Ardent Lover robb'd of all his Bliss,　　5
Not ancient Lady when refus'd a Kiss,
Not Tyrants fierce that unrepenting die,
Not *Cynthia* when her *Manteau*'s pinn'd awry,
E'er felt such Rage, Resentment, and Despair,
As Thou, sad Virgin! for thy ravish'd Hair.　　10
　While her rackt Soul Repose and Peace requires,
The fierce *Thalestris* fans the rising Fires.
O wretched Maid (she spreads her hands, and cry'd,
And *Hampton*'s Ecchoes, wretched Maid! reply'd)
Was it for this you took such constant Care,　　15
Combs, Bodkins, Leads, Pomatums, to prepare?
For this your Locks in Paper Durance bound,
For this with tort'ring Irons wreath'd around?
Oh had the Youth but been content to seize
Hairs less in sight – or any Hairs but these!　　20
Gods! shall the Ravisher display this Hair,
While the Fops envy, and the Ladies stare!
Honour forbid! at whose unrival'd Shrine
Ease, Pleasure, Virtue, All, our Sex resign.
Methinks already I your Tears survey,　　25
Already hear the horrid things they say,

Already see you a degraded Toast,
And all your Honour in a Whisper lost!
How shall I, then, your helpless Fame defend?
'Twill then be Infamy to seem your Friend!   30
And shall this Prize, th'inestimable Prize,
Expos'd thro' *Crystal* to the gazing Eyes,
And heighten'd by the *Diamond*'s circling Rays,
On that Rapacious Hand for ever blaze?
Sooner shall Grass in *Hide*-Park *Circus* grow,   35
And Wits take Lodgings in the Sound of *Bow*;
Sooner let Earth, Air, Sea, to *Chaos* fall,
Men, Monkies, Lap-dogs, Parrots, perish all!
    She said; then raging to *Sir Plume* repairs,
And bids her *Beau* demand the precious Hairs: 40
(*Sir Plume*, of *Amber Snuff-box* justly vain,
And the nice Conduct of a *clouded Cane*)
With earnest Eyes, and round unthinking Face,
He first the Snuff-box open'd, then the Case,
And thus broke out – 'My Lord, why, what the Devil?   45
'Z——ds! damn the Lock! 'fore Gad, you must be civil!
'Plague on't! 'tis past a Jest – nay prithee, Pox!
'Give her the Hair' – he spoke, and rapp'd his Box.
    It grieves me much (reply'd the Peer again)
Who speaks so well shou'd ever speak in vain.   50
But by this Locke, this sacred Locke I swear,
(Which never more shall join its parted Hair,
Which never more its Honours shall renew,
Clipt from the lovely Head where once it grew)
That while my Nostrils draw the vital Air,   55
This Hand, which won it, shall for ever wear.
He spoke, and speaking in proud Triumph spread

51 *In allusion to* Achilles*'s Oath in* Homer, Iliad, i. (P)

The long-contended Honours of her Head.

But see! the *Nymph* in Sorrow's Pomp appears,
Her Eyes half languishing, half drown'd in Tears;   60
Now livid pale her Cheeks, now glowing red; ⎫
On her heav'd Bosom hung her drooping Head, ⎬
Which, with a Sigh, she rais'd; and thus she said. ⎭

For ever curs'd be this detested Day,
Which snatch'd my best, my fav'rite Curl away!   65
Happy! ah ten times happy, had I been,
If *Hampton-Court* these Eyes had never seen!
Yet am not I the first mistaken Maid,
By Love of Courts to num'rous Ills betray'd.
Oh had I rather un-admir'd remain'd   70
In some lone *Isle*, or distant *Northern* Land;
Where the gilt *Chariot* never mark'd the way,
Where none learn *Ombre*, none e'er taste *Bohea*!
There kept my Charms conceal'd from mortal Eye,
Like Roses that in Desarts bloom and die.   75
What mov'd my Mind with youthful Lords to rome?
O had I stay'd, and said my Pray'rs at home!
'Twas this, the Morning *Omens* did foretel;
Thrice from my trembling hand the *Patch-box* fell;
The tott'ring *China* shook without a Wind,   80
Nay, *Poll* sate mute, and *Shock* was *most Unkind*!
See the poor Remnants of this slighted Hair!
My hands shall rend what ev'n thy own did spare.
This, in two sable Ringlets taught to break,
Once gave new Beauties to the snowie Neck.   85
The Sister-Locke now sits uncouth, alone,
And in its Fellow's Fate foresees its own;
Uncurl'd it hangs! the fatal Sheers demands;
And tempts once more thy sacrilegious Hands.

She said: the pitying Audience melt in Tears,   90
But *Fate* and *Jove* had stopp'd the *Baron*'s Ears.
In vain *Thalestris* with Reproach assails,
For who can move when fair *Belinda* fails?
Not half so fixt the *Trojan* cou'd remain,
While *Anna* begg'd and *Dido* rag'd in vain.   95
To Arms, to Arms! the bold *Thalestris* cries,
And swift as Lightning to the Combate flies.
All side in Parties, and begin th'Attack;
Fans clap, Silks russle, and tough Whalebones crack;
Heroes' and Heroins' Shouts confus'dly rise,   100
And base, and treble Voices strike the Skies.
No common Weapons in their Hands are found,
Like Gods they fight, nor dread a mortal Wound.

So when bold *Homer* makes the Gods engage,
And heavn'ly Breasts with human Passions rage;   105
'Gainst *Pallas*, *Mars*; *Latona*, *Hermes* Arms;
And all *Olympus* rings with loud Alarms.
Jove's Thunder roars, Heav'n trembles all around;
Blue *Neptune* storms, the bellowing Deeps resound;
Earth shakes her nodding Tow'rs, the Ground gives
            way,   110
And the pale Ghosts start at the Flash of Day!
    While thro' the Press enrag'd *Thalestris* flies,
And scatters Death around from both her Eyes,
A *Beau* and *Witling* perish'd in the Throng,
One dy'd in *Metaphor*, and one in *Song*.   115
O cruel Nymph! a living Death I bear,
Cry'd *Dapperwit*, and sunk beside his Chair.
A mournful Glance Sir *Fopling* upwards cast,
Those Eyes are made so killing – was his last:

104 Homer, *Iliad*, 20. (P)

D

Thus on *Meander's* flow'ry Margin lies   120
Th'expiring Swan, and as he sings he dies.

   As bold Sir *Plume* had drawn *Clarissa* down,
Chloë stept in, and kill'd him with a Frown;
She smil'd to see the doughty Hero slain,
But at her Smile, the Beau reviv'd again.   125

   Now *Jove* suspends his golden Scales in Air,
Weighs the Men's Wits against the Lady's Hair;
The doubtful Beam long nods from side to side;
At length the Wits mount up, the Hairs subside.

   See fierce *Belinda* on the *Baron* flies,   130
With more than usual Lightning in her Eyes;
   Nor fear'd the Chief th'unequal Fight to try,
Who sought no more than on his Foe to die.
But this bold Lord, with manly Strength indu'd,
She with one Finger and a Thumb subdu'd: 135
Just where the Breath of Life his Nostrils drew,
A Charge of *Snuff* the wily Virgin threw;
Sudden, with starting Tears each Eye o'erflows,
And the high Dome re-ecchoes to his Nose.

   Now meet thy Fate, th'incens'd Virago cry'd,   140
And drew a deadly *Bodkin* from her Side.
Boast not my Fall (he said) insulting Foe!
Thou by some other shalt be laid as low.
Nor think, to dye dejects my lofty Mind;
All that I dread, is leaving you behind!   145
Rather than so, ah let me still survive,
And still burn on, in *Cupid's* Flames, *Alive*.

   Restore the Locke! she cries, and all around
Restore the Locke! the vaulted Roofs rebound.
Not fierce *Othello* in so loud a Strain   150

126 *Vid.* Homer, *Iliad*, 22 and Virgil *Æneid*, 12. (P)

Roar'd for the Handkerchief that caus'd his Pain.
But see! how oft Ambitious Aims are cross'd,
And Chiefs contend 'till all the Prize is lost!
The Locke, obtain'd with Guilt, and kept with Pain,
In ev'ry place is sought, but sought in vain: 155
With such a Prize no Mortal must be blest,
So Heav'n decrees! with Heav'n who can contest?
    Some thought, it mounted to the Lunar Sphere,
Since all that Man e'er lost, is treasur'd there.
There Heroes' Wits are kept in pondrous Vases,   160
And Beaus' in *Snuff-boxes* and *Tweezer-Cases*.
There broken Vows, and Death-bed Alms are found,
And Lovers' Hearts with Ends of Riband bound;
The Courtier's Promises, and Sick Man's Pray'rs,
The Smiles of Harlots, and Tears of Heirs,   165
Cages for Gnats, and Chains to Yoak a Flea;
Dry'd Butterflies, and Tomes of Casuistry.
    But trust the Muse – she saw it upward rise,
Tho' mark'd by none but quick Poetic Eyes:
(Thus *Rome*'s great Founder to the Heavn's withdrew,   170
To *Proculus* alone confess'd in view.)
A sudden Star, it shot thro' liquid Air,
And drew behind a radiant *Trail of Hair*.
Not *Berenice*'s Locks first rose so bright,
The Skies bespangling with dishevel'd Light.   175
This, the *Beau-monde* shall from the *Mall* survey,⎫
As thro' the Moon-light shade they nightly stray,⎬
And hail with Musick its propitious Ray.⎭
This *Partridge* soon shall view in cloudless Skies,
When next he looks thro' *Galilæo*'s Eyes;   180
And hence th'Egregious Wizard shall foredoom

159 *Vid.* Ariosto, Canto 34. (P)

The Fate of *Louis*, and the Fall of *Rome*.

   Then cease, bright Nymph! to mourn the ravish'd Hair
Which adds new Glory to the shining Sphere!
Not all the Tresses that fair Head can boast   185
Shall draw such Envy as the Locke you lost.
For, after all the Murders of your Eye,
When, after Millions slain, your self shall die;
When those fair Suns shall sett, as sett they must,
And all those Tresses shall be laid in Dust;   190
This Locke, the Muse shall consecrate to Fame,
And mid'st the Stars inscribe *Belinda*'s Name!

FINIS

APPENDIX B

SYLPHS

In the second edition of the *Rape of the Lock*, Pope enlarged the two cantos to five and did this mainly by adding to the machinery. His choice of supernaturals shows how alive he was to literature which could not be counted on to help him to be a poet – for he found his sylphs in *Le Conte de Gabalis*, a *roman* written forty years earlier in France by the Abbé de Montfaucon de Villars, and which had been twice translated into English. This short novel is itself a skit on the sylphs of a system, the Rosicrucian philosophy, which had been inaugurated in Germany a hundred years earlier. It would have been a weakness in Pope's poem if he had had to invent these machines, since the machinery of the serious epic derived from established mythology; and the 'mythology' of the Rosicrucians was known well enough to count as established.

Pope, then, owed to *Gabalis* the right to assume the existence of this particular system of elemental sprites. The novel lays it down that:

the *Elements* are inhabited by most Perfect Creatures; from the Knowledge and Commerce of whom, the Sin of the Unfortunate *Adam*, has excluded all his too Unhappy Posterity. This immense Space, which is between the Earth, and the *Heavens*, has more Noble Inhabitants, than *Birds* and *Flyes*: This vast Ocean has also other Troops, besides *Dolphins* and *Whales*: The Profundity of the Earth, is not only for *Moles*; And the *Element* of *Fire*, (more Noble than the other Three) was not made to be Unprofitable and Voyd.

The *Air* is full of an innumerable Multitude of People,

having Human Shape, somewhat Fierce in appearance, but Tractable upon experience . . . Their Wives, and their Daughters have a kind of Masculine Beauty, such as we describe the *Amazons* to have . . . the *Seas* and *Rivers* are Inhabited, as well as the *Air:* The Antient *Sages* have called these kind of People *Undians* or *Nymphs.* They have but few Males amongst them; but the Women are there in great Numbers: Their Beauty is marvellous; and the Daughters of Men have nothing in them, comparable to these.

The Earth is filled almost to the Center with *Gnomes* or *Pharyes*; a People of small Stature; the Guardians of Treasures, of Mines, and of Precious Stones. They are Ingenious, Friends of Men, and easie to be commanded . . .

As for the *Salamanders*, the Inhabitants of the Region of *Fire* . . . the *Idea*, which the ignorant Painters and Sculpters have given them [is wrong]: The Wives of the *Salamanders* are Fair; nay, rather more Fair, than all others, seeing they are of a purer Element . . .

Pope is obviously deeply indebted to such passages but he strengthens the appeal to 'established' mythology by adopting whatever he can use from other mythologies (especially when such adoption improves the epic mimicry) and by grafting the whole lot on 'all the Nurse and all the Priest have taught'.[1] The opinion, called a 'foolish' one by Burton, that 'angels and devils are nought but souls of men departed', allows him to give his sprites an appropriate pre-existence as human beings: and in taking over this item Pope improves the mock-heroics – the Elysian shades of Virgil and Ovid had found congenial occupations. Pope also borrows the opinion that transmigrated souls protect their friends on earth, and conspire against their enemies: he makes the sylphs guardians of maidens; and this again carries its epic

[1] *Rape of the Lock,* I 30 f.

reference since the epic heroes were provided with their divine guardians. In *Gabalis* all the sprites are 'good', but Pope, following the traditional categories of spirits, makes the gnomes 'bad', wickedly contriving such vexations as are exemplified at iv 67 ff.; this, again, makes them more like the factious celestials of the epics. The sylphs in *Gabalis* can change their shape and sex at will, and in adopting this detail Pope is also adopting from epic: Milton's angels 'Can either Sex assume, or both'. Like Milton's angels again, Pope's sylphs are invulnerable, since if their bodies are divided they can, in the words of Burton, 'with admirable celerity . . . come together again'.

On one occasion de Villars displays his sylphs in cosmic parade:

The famous Cabalist *Zedechias*, was moved in his Spirit, in the Reign of your King *Pepin*, to Convince the World, that the *Elements* are Inhabited by all these People, whose Nature I have been describing to you. The Expedient to bring all this about, was in this manner; He advised the *Sylphs* to shew themselves in the Air to all the World. They did it with great Magnificence: These Creatures appearing in the Air, in Human Shape; Sometimes ranged in Battle, Marching in good Order, or standing to their Arms, or Encamped under most Majestick Pavillions: At other times, on Airy Ships of an Admirable Structure, whose Flying Navy was tost about at the Will of the *Zephirus*'s . . . The People presently believed, that they were *Sorcerers*, who had gotten a Power in the Air, there to exercise their Conjurations, and to make it Hail upon their Corn-Fields . . . Being transported with the Fury which Inspired them with such Imaginations, they dragged these *Innocents* to Punishment. It is incredible, what a great Number of [sylphs] were made to suffer by Fire, and Water, all over this Kingdom.

Pope borrows the idea of regimentation: he writes 'The light *Militia* of the lower Sky', 'The lucid Squadrons', 'th' Aerial Guard', 'her Airy Band', 'Propt on their Bodkin Spears'.[1]

He is, however, more scientifically interested than de Villars in the living conditions of the sylphs and he goes for help to another French book, this time Fontenelle's *Pluralité de Mondes*. It is on the basis of the scientific whims of Fontenelle that Pope's fancy scrupulously builds up its universe. The following sentences from a contemporary translation may be compared with ii 77–86 of the poem:

the Earth which is solid, is covered from the surface 20 Leagues upwards, with a kind of Down, which is the Air . . . Beyond the Air is the Celestial Matter, incomparably more pure and subtile . . . This pale Light which comes to us from the Moon [is reflected light] . . . the Neighbouring Worlds sometimes send Visits to us, and that in a very magnificent and splendid manner: There come Comets to us from thence, adorn'd with Bright shining Hair, Venerable Beards, or Majestick Tails . . . Comets are nothing but Planets, which belong to a Neighbouring Vortex, they move towards the out-side of it; but perhaps this Vortex being differently press'd by those Vortex's which encompass it, it is rounder above than it is below, and it is the lower part that is still towards us. These Planets which have begun to move in a Circle above, are not aware that below their Vortex will fail 'em, because it is as it were broken. Therefore to continue the Circular Motion, it is necessary that they enter into another Vortex, which we will suppose is ours, and that they cut through the outsides of it. They appear to us very high, and are much higher than *Saturn*, and according to our System, it is absolutely necessary they should be so high . . . Their Beards and their Tails . . . are not real, they are

---

[1] *Id.*, i 42, ii 56, iii 31 and 113, v 55.

Phænomena, and but meer Appearances . . . our Air consists of thicker and grosser Vapours than the Air of the Moon . . . The Rainbow . . . is not known to them in the Moon; for if the Dawn is an effect of the grossness of the Air and Vapours, the Rainbow is form'd in the Clouds, from whence the Rain falls; [The inhabitants of the moon] have neither Thunder nor Lightning . . . how glorious are their days, the sun continually shining?

II

Pope's sylphs are, of course, more vividly realized than those of de Villars, and, in the same way that he rifles other systems to enrich the Rosicrucian mythology, he rifles earlier English poets to enrich the sylphs themselves. He takes hints and words from the Ariel of Shakespeare (perhaps as he appears in Dryden's version of the *Tempest*), the fairies and angels of Milton, and the fairies and demons of Dryden. Pope associates the sylphs and sylphids with their short vowel *i*. There are the names Brillante and Crispissa and the short *i* narrows the lip movements of several lines; for instance:

> Thin glitt'ring Textures of the filmy Dew;
> Dipt in the richest Tincture of the Skies . . .
> Or dip their Pinions in the painted Bow . . .
> Some thrid the mazy Ringlets of her Hair . . .

The vowel springs most plentifully when Ariel threatens torments:

> . . . transfixt with *Pins* . . .
> . . . *Stypticks* . . .
> Shrink his thin Essence like a rivell'd Flower.
> Or as *Ixion* fix'd, the Wretch shall feel
> The giddy Motion of the whirling Mill.

Other poets beside Pope have associated their fairies with the short *i*. There are the names (Pip, Trip, Skip, Fib, Tib, etc.) of Drayton's fairies, and those of Herrick's fairy saints (Tit, Nit, Is, Will o' the Wispe, Frip, Trip, Fill, Fillie). The associations of Pope's fairies reach forward to the insects in the satires and to such a phrase as 'the Cynthia of this minute'.

Pope's originality most obviously shows itself in the way he particularizes the notions he has borrowed (see, e.g., the account of the sylphs' guardianship of maidens, i 71 ff.), and in the feminine satire which salts much of what he says of them and much of what he makes them say. In other poets fairies are country creatures.

APPENDIX C

THE HEROIC COUPLET

When we read the *Rape of the Lock* we are conscious of a firmly controlled progression. The poet is master, he has put things just so.

The poem performs a lively but stately solo dance, performs it without jerk, however often the pace may change.[1] But though the dance is kept moving towards the conclusion of the story, it fascinates us by its subsidiary footwork as well as by its progression, by the footwork which does not so much break new ground as decorate a small area, as in pirouetting. For the unit, the poem, is made up of subsidiary units (i.e., of parts which, when isolated, invite temporary consideration as things complete in themselves). These subsidiary units are, in order of descending size, the canto, the paragraph, the couplet, even the line, even the phrase.

The following remarks mainly concern the couplet.

I

The heroic couplet, as Pope wrote it, attracts attention to itself as metre. It is so brief that, as we read, we notice variations between couplets in something like the same way that we notice variations between dominos all of which are of the same size. We do not compare metrical units always: for example, when reading the *Faërie Queene* we do not compare stanzas; we anticipate and value the metre within

[1] The question whether or not the pace may dally sometimes is canvassed in the Introduction, at p. 19 above.

the stanza, but the stanzas nine lines long are too big to be held in the mind as comparable units. But variety among Pope's couplets cannot well be missed.

Heroic couplets had not always been written in the way Pope wrote them. He may be said to have regarded them as if they were stanzas, self-contained; or, if not quite that, as having a beginning, middle and end even though at the end stood a gate and a gate which on some occasions he opened to allow the sense to drive through. That is, the couplet may belong to the paragraph, even more than to itself: but if so, it is only because Pope deliberately chose to open the gate.

Many of Pope's couplets may be taken out of their contexts and held up to separate admiration like an occasional lyric stanza, or figurative stanza, from the *Faërie Queene*. For example, at random from *Windsor Forest*:

> Thy shady empire shall retain no trace
> Of war or blood, but in the sylvan chase;

from the *Epilogue to the Satires*:

> Yes, I am proud; I must be proud to see
> Men not afraid of God, afraid of me;

from the *Epistle to Arbuthnot*:

> Pains, reading, study are their just pretence,
> And all they want is spirit, taste, and sense;

from the *Dunciad*:

> So clouds, replenish'd from some bog below,
> Mount in dark volumes, and descend in snow.

These and a thousand more are satisfying as complete stanzas, and there is no doubt that Pope looked on the couplet as capable of attaining a temporary unity in itself. He took up

this attitude the more readily because of the metrical dis-
coveries of those fashionable poets of the later seventeenth
century – Waller and Dryden in particular – who had already
changed the nature of the heroic couplet.

Among the Elizabethans and some later poets – Chaucer
may be left out of account since corrupt texts prevented
seventeenth-century readers from discovering that his
couplets were regular – the couplet had resembled loose
blank verse bedropped with rime. Here are some of their
couplets on a theme near to the *Rape of the Lock*:

> A vain inconstant dame, that counts her loves
> By this enamell'd ring, that pair of gloves,
> And with her chamber-maid when closely set,
> Turning her letters in her cabinet,
> Makes known what tokens have been sent unto her,
> What man did bluntly, who did courtly woo her;
> Who hath the best face, neatest leg, most lands,
> Who for his carriage in her favour stands.
> Op'ning her paper then she shows her wit
> On an epistle that some fool had writ:
> Then meeting with another which she likes,
> Her chambermaid's great reading quickly strikes
> That good opinion dead, and swears that this
> Was stol'n from Palmerin or Amadis.[1]

The unit of such metre is the long sentence or paragraph.
Even where Pope's couplets are not units, even where, that
is, they are meaninglessly incomplete without their fellows,
they are much more nearly units than most of these couplets
of William Browne's. And being units or near-units, the
variety between them is seized on as valuable in a way that,
in the couplets of William Browne, it is not.

[1] William Browne, *Fido: An Epistle to Fidelia*, 93 ff.

II

Here are a few of Pope's couplets chosen to show how various their configuration may be:

(1) The *Gnomes* direct, to ev'ry Atome just,
    The pungent Grains of titillating Dust.   (v 83 f.)

(2) Sooner let Earth, Air, Sea, to *Chaos* fall,
    Men, Monkies, Lap-dogs, Parrots, perish all!   (iv 119 f.)

(3) The Courtier's Promises, and Sick Man's Pray'rs,
    The Smiles of Harlots, and the Tears of Heirs.   (v 119 f.)

(4) Or stain her Honour, or her new Brocade,
    Forget her Pray'rs, or miss a Masquerade.   (ii 107 f.)

We notice in these couplets different structures, ranging from simple to complicated. When we look into the more complicated ones, we see that, as well as being complete in themselves, they are themselves formed of parts, of detachable phrases; and that these parts are sometimes strips parallel and sometimes strips crossed.

No. (3) is an example of parallel strips. If, as Euclid would say, 'The Courtier's Promises' is a line AB and the 'Sick Man's Pray'rs' a line CD: then, if the paper is folded down the middle, CD will lie along AB. Similarly with the two parts of the second line of couplet No. 3. No. 4, however, is a different matter. In that couplet we can separate out the following strips:

(*a*) 'Or stain her Honour'
(*b*) 'or her new Brocade'.
(*c*) 'Forget her Pray'rs'
(*d*) 'or miss a Masquerade'.

We may say, first of all, that (*a*) + (*b*) is parallel to (*c*) + (*d*). We may also say that (*a*) is parallel to (*b*), and (*c*) to (*d*). But we note that, while $(a) + (b)$ is parallel to $(c) + (d)$ on two counts, first as sound and general construction, and second as meaning, (a) is parallel to (b) as sound, and (c) to (d), but (a) is contrary to (b) as meaning and (c) to (d). If we read these lines carelessly, mainly for the sound, we find them similar to the lines of couplet No. 3 above. And then we see that carelessness has tricked us! The sound, the syntax, says one thing, the meaning another and, our carelessness shaken off, the similarity in the sound acts like a catapult projecting us full against the satiric meaning. The sound says: 'Young ladies think these things, (a) and (b), (c) and (d), are the same things: they distinguish no difference in value.' The meaning says: 'No things could be more different than (a) and (b), (c) and (d).' And when sound and meaning unite their voices, they say: 'These things are different, though young ladies slur over the differences.' Pope's meaning is often achieved through his metre as much as through his words. Or to put it more exactly: Pope, seeing the value of conciseness, saw also that the heroic couplet – that of all metres – could be patterned and rhythm'd so as to save words, so as to complete the subtlety of a meaning which otherwise would have taken up more space. The metre whispers to the reader the sense, the tone, the nuance which those words have not needed to be used for. Pope laughed at poetry which puts its readers to sleep and he relies partly on his metre to keep readers awake, to enlist that collaboration which clears the air of stupor.

APPENDIX D

THE LIFE OF POPE

Mr. John Butt, the General Editor of the *Twickenham Pope*, has kindly supplied the following biography [ED.].

Alexander Pope was born on 21 May 1688 in the city of London, where his father is believed to have worked in the wholesale linen trade. Nothing is known for certain of the boy's early years, except that his physique was never good. As the result of too much study (so he thought), he acquired a curvature of the spine and some tubercular infection, which limited his growth – his full-grown height was four feet six inches – and seriously impaired his health. He struggled to ignore these handicaps – and indeed he could honestly protest at times that he was

> The gayest valetudinaire,
>   Most thinking rake, alive, –

but it was inevitable that his deformity and his poor health should interfere with his activities throughout what he pathetically calls 'this long Disease, my Life', and should increase his sensitiveness to mental and physical pain.

Pope's parents left London to live at Binfield in Windsor Forest when their son was about twelve years old. They made this move, in all probability, because they were Roman Catholics, for to be a Catholic at this time was to lay oneself open to suspicion and persecution. Several laws were passed forbidding Catholics to live within ten miles of London, preventing their children from being taught by Catholic priests, and compelling them to forfeit two-thirds of their estates or the value thereof. And of course they were prevented from serving in Parliament or holding any office of profit under the Crown. Though these laws were not always rigorously enforced, a political crisis such as the '15 rebellion might well serve to remind the Government of its powers. When studying the life or the works of Pope, we cannot long forget that he was a Catholic. His parents thought it was best to live out of London, and he himself found it inadvisable to come up to town for medical attention during his last illness. At a time when most men of letters were employed by one or other political party, Pope was one of the few who derived no income from party funds. His poem *Messiah* recalls the phraseology of the Catholic translation of the Bible rather than the phraseology of the Anglican 'Authorized Version'; his *Eloisa to Abelard* reads like the work of a Catholic; and *The Rape of the Lock* was intended to reconcile two Catholic families. One of Pope's less pleasing characteristics, his habit of equivocating – that is, not actually telling lies, but wording his statements so as to give a false impression – was the self-defensive weapon of the Jesuits. And if he had been an Anglican, his schooling would probably have been more formal and extensive. As it was, he was mainly self-educated, though he attended one or two Catholic schools for short periods. He was a precocious boy, an eager reader in several languages which he managed to teach himself, and an incessant scribbler, turning out verse upon verse in imitation of the poets he read. The best of these earliest writings are the famous *Ode on Solitude* and a paraphrase of St. Thomas à Kempis, both of which, so he said, were written at the age of twelve. But perhaps in later life he imagined himself to have been even more precocious than he actually was.

Though his home was in Windsor Forest, Pope must frequently have been in London, since before he was twenty he had begun to make friends with many of the chief men of letters of the day, such as Congreve, Wycherley, Garth, and Walsh. With Walsh, whom Dryden had called 'the best critic of our nation', he entered into correspondence on the subject of versification, and to Congreve and others he showed the manuscript of his *Pastorals*, which a few years later (1709) were to become his first published work. The nine years from 1708 to 1717 were experimental years for Pope. He was busy attempting a variety of poetical 'kinds' to try where his strength lay. Following in the steps of Boileau (and, of course, of Horace) he tried his hand at a poem about the writing of poetry, and produced the *Essay on Criticism* (1711). Boileau's *Le Lutrin* (1674) and Garth's *Dispensary* (1699) suggested to him the idea of a mock epic, which he fulfilled in *The Rape of the Lock* (1712). And with Denham's *Coopers Hill* (1642) in mind, he attempted a 'local poem', a 'kind' in which the landscape to be described recalls historic and other associations; this poem, called *Windsor Forest*, was published in 1713. Two of many more experiments may be mentioned – the *Eloisa to Abelard*, an imitation of Ovid's *Heroical Epistles*, and the *Elegy to the Memory of an Unfortunate Lady*, modelled on the elegies of Ovid and Tibullus.

These last two poems were published in 1717 in a collected volume of his poems. This beautifully printed book contains some of Pope's very best work, the perfect revised version of *The Rape of the Lock*, the famous proverbs of the *Essay on Criticism*, the exquisitely musical versification of the *Pastorals*; but none the less it is a volume of experiments. Pope now knew where his strength lay. Looking back on these experiments in his later years, he was accustomed to make a distinction between these earlier 'fanciful' poems and his mature work in which he wrote of 'Truth' and 'the Heart'. This was a deliberate change, a deliberate canalizing of his poetical powers. From henceforth, with the exception of his translation of Homer, Social Comment and Social Philosophy were to be his theme. But this theme is already to be found in parts of the 1717 volume, and nowhere better than in 'the grave Clarissa's' speech, vv. 9–34 of the 5th canto of *The Rape of the Lock.*

By this time (1717), Pope was recognized as the foremost poet of his day. He had made a wide circle of friends in London, and several enemies as well. With Swift, whom he had met about the year 1712, with Gay, Dr Arbuthnot, the Earl of Oxford, and others, he formed the Scriblerus Club, whose members met (until 1714) to compose joint satires on pedantry and false learning. He also knew Steele and Addison. But though he admired Addison's work, Pope could never become intimate with him. They were temperamentally antipathetic. Addison, the slightly self-conscious model of literary decorum, was often offended by the indiscretions of the brilliant younger man. And Pope disliked being patronized as much as Addison liked patronizing. Some not quite straightforward behaviour on Addison's part in supporting a rival translation of Homer, and some hypersensitiveness on Pope's part provoked the famous 'character' which Pope sent to Addison and later printed as a character of Atticus in the *Epistle to Dr. Arbuthnot.*

The translation of Homer was now absorbing all his energies. The first four books of the *Iliad* were published in 1715, and the translation was completed in 1720. The *Odyssey,* for which he enlisted the help of Broome and

Fenton, was published in five volumes in 1725 and 1726. The Homer of Pope's translation is powdered and peri-wigged, but that is not more than to say that Pope was translating him to suit the taste of the times, as Chapman had previously translated him to suit the taste of the Elizabethans. Pope's version, in spite of its faults of taste and scholarship, remains the most readable of our translations of Homer.

The labour had been great, but the reward was great, too. No poem had ever sold so well before. Pope's financial position was secured.

> 'Thanks to Homer,' he wrote, 'I live and thrive
> Indebted to no Prince or Peer alive.'

Pope and his parents had moved from Binfield to Chiswick in 1716, where his father died in the following year. In 1718 he and his mother rented a villa on the Thames at Twickenham, in those days still a small country town where several Londoners retired to live in rustic seclusion. This was to be Pope's home for the remaining twenty-six years of his life. Here he entertained such friends as Swift and Bolingbroke with studied modesty, regaling them on gudgeons and flounders from the Thames at his door and on figs and walnuts from the little garden which he took such pains to design and cultivate. He kept his own boatman to row him down-stream on his frequent visits to London, and his own coach to take him on his round of summer visits to country friends, such as Lord Bathurst at Cirencester, Lord Cobham at Stowe, Ralph Allen the philanthropist at Prior Park near Bath, and Lord Peterborough at Southampton. All these friends were enthusiastic gardeners, too; and it was one of Pope's greatest pleasures to advise and superintend the laying out of the grounds on the best romantic principles. A seat at Cirencester, a fantastic grotto and an ivy-mantled tower at Prior Park still bear Pope's name.

Having presented Homer, the greatest of the Ancients, to his contemporaries, Pope next turned his attention to the greatest of the Moderns and produced an elegant edition of Shakespeare in 1725. It is not a good edition by our modern standards, for Pope had treated Shakespeare much as he treated Homer; he had made him conform to modern standards of taste – in some degree, at any rate – by removing the more obvious blemishes which Shakespeare had committed. Some of Pope's contemporaries had not approved of his translation of Homer – 'It is a pretty poem, Mr. Pope', the great scholar, Bentley, had remarked, 'but you must not call it Homer.' And now disapproval was expressed of the edition of Shakespeare. In particular a scholar named Theobald exposed its deficiencies in a book called *Shakespeare Restored*. Pope was peculiarly sensitive to such attacks upon his work – and to attacks upon his character – of which many had been published during the past fifteen years. Dennis, a friend of Dryden and a critic of some repute, had published a damaging series of *Remarks* on most of Pope's publications, having been spurred to do so by an indiscreet allusion to his irascibility which Pope had slipped into the *Essay on Criticism* (ll. 585 ff.). And many smaller fry had joined in to bait him. Pope was now determined to repay them. He was smarting under these attacks. Of that there is no doubt. But he comforted himself by reflecting that he was maintaining the highest literary standards and that his enemies were pedants and other persons devoid of spirit, taste, and sense. This is the line of defence which he assumed in *The Dunciad* (1728), a mock-epic like *The Rape of the Lock*, but more sombre, often more magnificent, and less easily appreciated. To make his satire on pedantry the sharper, he reissued the poem in 1729 with an elaborate mock-commentary of prefaces, notes, appendices, indexes, and errata, as a burlesque of scholarship. In his poem his enemies are preserved like flies in amber. We need notes to-day to discover who they were, but even without notes it is not difficult to see what defects and stupidities these poor wretches represent.

In the winter of 1730, Pope told his friend Spence of a new work which he was contemplating. It was to be a series of verse epistles, of which the first four or five would be on 'The Nature of Man' and the rest would be on Moderation or 'the Use of Things'. This work was never completed, but though Pope was more than once deflected from it, he never abandoned the intention till the end of his life. An epistle from one of the later sections was the first to be published. This was *Of Taste* (1731), now known as *Moral Essay, Epistle IV*, and was addressed to his friend, Lord Burlington, the famous amateur architect. This poem, which is one of the most characteristic works of Pope's maturity, presents an entertaining selection of examples of false taste in architecture and landscape gardening, and concludes with some suggestions for a worthier use of money. Within the next four years three more *Moral Essays* were published as well as a group of four epistles entitled *An Essay on Man*, which was intended to serve as the introduction to the larger work which Pope had in view. The *Moral Essays*, with their brilliant observations of human nature, provide better reading than the *Essay on Man*, in which Pope is concerned to vindicate the doctrine that 'whatever is, is right'. But the reader of the *Essay on Man* will be rewarded by finding much that is beautiful and much proverbial wisdom that 'springs eternal in the human breast'; he will surely enjoy

the stately opening of the second epistle, which recalls
Hamlet's 'What a piece of work is Man' but without any
fear of what the comparison may reveal.

Meanwhile Pope was being deflected from his great work.
An outcry had been raised against *Of Taste* by persons who
thought they recognized the Duke of Chandos, a generous
subscriber to Pope's Homer, under the pseudonym of Timon,
an example of a tasteless magnifico. It has recently been
shown that Pope could not have meant Timon to represent
Chandos; but certain features sufficiently resembled him, and
so when Pope protested his innocence he was not believed.
This attack and others of a similar nature caused him to think
out his position as a satirist, and to ponder the ethics of
writing satire. The form his defence took was to 'imitate'
the first satire of the second book of Horace, itself a defence
of satire; that is to say, he loosely translated this satire, sub-
stituting modern parallels for contemporary allusions in the
original. In this poem, in the *Epistle to Dr. Arbuthnot* (1735),
a further defence of himself and his writings, and in the
Epilogue to the Satires (1738), his last word on the subject,
Pope contended that the satirist's duty is to uphold a standard
of moral rectitude and to point out deviations from that
standard by chastising the most notorious and powerful
offenders, those men who

> Safe from the Bar, the Pulpit, and the Throne
> (are) Yet touch'd and sham'd by *Ridicule* alone.

To choose living examples was he thought best. Sometimes
their identity was partially concealed under the anonymity
of a 'Sappho' – such names may even represent types rather
than individuals – and sometimes they appear without
disguise. Undoubtedly Pope used his satire to repay the

attacks of his personal enemies. But we should not assume too hastily that all who are exposed had given Pope some personal cause for offence. The majority are flagrant offenders against the high standards of behaviour which Pope is advocating, just as Mr Murphy and the Rev. W. Cattle, who appear in the pages of *Culture and Anarchy*, were not the personal enemies of Matthew Arnold but the enemies which Culture had to fight.

Pope's standards are expounded and defended not only in the *Moral Essays* but in a series of *Imitations of Horace* (1733–8) to which he was prompted by the success of the first Imitation mentioned above. These standards were the old Horatian standards of Temperance, of Contentment with a modest Competence. A man should make a charitable and tasteful use of such money as he possesses, as the Man of Ross had done (*Moral Es.*, iii 249 ff.), or as Bathurst or Burlington were doing. He should be able, like Bethel (2nd *Imit. Hor.*), to find within himself or ready at hand whatever is necessary to divert his leisure. Above all he must cultivate an honest, open-hearted, and serene disposition. Pope himself was not completely successful in living up to this standard. Too often he allowed his serenity to be ruffled by the vicious attacks of his enemies; and some of his actions, noably his procuring that a 'stolen' edition of his letters should be printed in order that he might modestly issue an authorized edition, can only be characterized as oblique. But no reader of his poetry can doubt that these standards were very real to him, and no student of the letters and memoirs of the time can fail to recognize the deep respect in which he was held both as a man and as a poet by the great men of his day whom he numbered amongst his friends.

The pedant and the hack writer had been the main objects

of Pope's attack in *The Dunciad*. In these later poems his attack is mainly directed against debauchery and corruption, those vices which the temperate and open-hearted man most cordially abhors. The corrupting power of money is constantly Pope's theme. And as time goes on he becomes more and more certain that political corruption is the source of all other corruption. The materialistic standards of the commercially minded Whigs, the bribing of Parliamentary electors, the horse laugh at honesty, the contempt of the patriot, when this state of affairs is encouraged by Walpole and his government, it is no wonder that higher standards cannot prevail, and that

> with the silent growth of ten per Cent,
> In Dirt and Darkness hundreds stink content.

In the *Imitations of Horace*, therefore, and in the *Epilogue to the Satires*, political satire becomes of growing importance; and it is political satire directed not merely by Pope's inward conviction but by his friend Bolingbroke, who had returned from exile to conduct the opposition to Walpole. In the last years of the seventeen-thirties, Pope had gathered round him all the most promising members of this opposition, and he had become their poet laureate.

He lived to see Walpole's fall from power, but he had ceased writing political satire with the *Epilogue*, because, as he said, 'Ridicule was become as unsafe as it was ineffectual'. He thought of returning to the *Essay of Man* once more, but he was deflected from it once again by a task to which he had always given much deliberation, the correction of his poetry. *The Dunciad* was enlarged by the addition of a fourth book (1742) and thoroughly revised (1743), Theobald being dethroned and another enemy, Colley Cibber, the actor-dramatist, being set up to rule the Dunces in his stead. Changes of a less momentous nature were being made in other poems, but Pope did not live long enough to see them all published. He died of an asthmatical dropsy on 30 May 1744, in his fifty-sixth year.

SUGGESTIONS FOR FURTHER READING

G. Sherburn, *The Early Career of Alexander Pope* (1934)

G. Tillotson, *On the Poetry of Pope* (1938, revised 1950)

M. Mack, 'Wit and Poetry and Pope', in *Pope and his Contemporaries: Essays presented to George Sherburn* (1949)

Ian Jack, *Augustan Satire* (1952)

J. Butt (ed.), *The Poems of Alexander Pope* (1963), a one-volume edition of The Twickenham Pope